10/25/04

Best Wishes
to the Sherwood Library

Louise Weeble

Dearest Darling Wife . . .

Just a Few Lines To Let

You Know I Am Okay

A Soldier's Letters To Home

Louise Weible

ISBN : Hardcover 1-4134-5246-9
Softcover 1-4134-5245-0

This book was printed in the United States of America.

To order additional copies of this book, contact:
Xlibris Corporation
1-888-795-4274
www.Xlibris.com
Orders@Xlibris.com
24439

CONTENTS

Dedication

I dedicate this book to my mother and father who lived their lives in such a way that it impels me to attempt to relate their story of how their lives began with each other.

Most of all I dedicate this book to Dad, not only to honor him but also to thank him. He met and fell in love with a young divorced woman with three small children. And in doing so, he made promises. He kept those promises. He was our hero. He still is.

Introduction

I have always been fascinated by the stories that Mom, mostly, told over the years, of the romantic way that she and Dad met, courted, and married. I was also captivated by her stories, after she had traveled to "magical" California so they could be together until the time came for Dad to be shipped overseas. No one knew when or even if this would happen because of the "loose lips, sinks ships", admonition.

But when the signs and rumors indicated that it was imminent that Dad would be going overseas soon, he arranged for Mom and we children to move to Ohio from Tennessee. In his heart, that is where he wanted to return to; although he "let" Mom make that decision. From his letters, he can be seen gently persuading her, even though he always reiterated that it was entirely "up to her" . . . or "what was her view?" And "they both could decide what was best. etc."

I also believe from reading these letters that he wanted to remove Mom from close proximity to her ex-spouse.

These letters will speak of how their love developed, from the time they met, until Dad's return from the war. They experienced reluctance from both sides of the families. Mom's father was very nervous about what he almost considered her marrying a foreigner, from "up north". In this agitated state, when Mom spanked Jr., her older child, about a lie she thought he had told, Grandpa turned Mom over his knee and spanked her.

She was shocked and swore it was the first and only time he had ever raised his hand to her. Dad was there at the time and startled to say the least. Throughout his letters, he teases her about "getting a spanking" in reference to that incident.

Dad's mother resisted the idea that her "favorite son" had suddenly married a divorced woman who already had three children, and from the south, no less. I think she believed Mom had caught him with her womanly wiles at a vulnerable time. Reading the letters will disprove that . . . to a point, anyway. Dad's sister said Grandma was like a "thunderbolt" when she got the news. And although she did not think much of the south in general, she once harshly corrected a woman who commented that we kids would be alright after we had learned to speak English. Grandma retorted hotly that we spoke better English than her German accented English.

As the letters unfold, they will tell you what happened; except for the year she was in California with him. Any letters he may have sent to us then, have been lost. I have tried to cover some of that year in this introduction. Otherwise, the letters he wrote, spoke of longings, insecurities, intense homesickness, jealousies, humor, their future, etc; and yes, some manipulation; all for the best, of course. It also speaks of what we recognize today as historical events.

Dad was close enough to the combat zone that he was blown out a window when a bomb landed nearby.

Dad saw the concentration camps and starving Germans, including children. I can attest to the fact that these traumas affected him the rest of his life. He told of one Christmas when the whole camp waited for their dinner until all the people and children, hanging around the garbage bins outside the kitchen scrounging for food scraps, had been brought in for the first table sitting and fed. They happened to be German. He could never abide waste after that.

He did not speak of the "oven" at the concentration camp to me until he was on his deathbed. He rambled on about the "pretty painted French carts and the oven that went on and on through the brick wall". I thought he was hallucinating about his army cooking days until I saw a documentary about the concentration camps and saw an oven that went on and on through a brick wall. My sister told me later that he had spoken of them to her one night when she had returned home from a date and found him crying. I know he suffered periodic nervous episodes that today we recognize as post-traumatic syndrome. Just before he was to return to the United States at the end of the war, he was convinced to sign on for another thirty days and be paid more money to do so. I have either read or saw in a documentary of sorts that General Eisenhower had wanted soldiers to see the concentration camps so that there would be witnesses to that monstrous deed. He did not want history to be reinvented or rewritten on that particular point. Perhaps that was the reason for Dad's thirty-day extension of duty. He spoke so little of the war that it did not even seem to exist for him. I believe that like most soldiers, he just wanted to come home and live an ordinary life and forget.

These letters will tell of a naïve young woman leaving her home state of Tennessee for the first time and traveling on a train across the nation to be with her new husband at Dillon Beach, near Petaluma, California. Upon reaching a certain destination where she would have to transfer to a bus to continue her journey, she found that the bus would not arrive until the next morning. Afraid to venture out on her own in a strange and overwhelming city, she settled down to spend the night in the station, sitting or sleeping on the hard benches, if need be.

A Special Military Patrol came by, told her that the station closed at two o'clock a.m. and she would have to move on at that time. She didn't know what to do or where to go, so he offered to let her walk patrol with him until they could figure out what to do until the station opened up again. After an hour or so, Mom asked if there would be an all night theater in the area. He didn't know but they walked and looked until they found one. Mom went in there to spend the night. She said the S.M.P. came in several times to check on her and came back for a final time to escort her back to the station when it finally opened. She never forgot his kindness.

She also told of another incident where she and a girl friend spotted something dark and long floating on the ocean. Since fear of enemy submarines sailing too close to our shores prevailed, people were asked to be on alert at all times for anything that looked suspicious and report it to the authorities. It was discovered that it was only a log riding the waves. While they were somewhat embarrassed at this revelation, they were commended for their diligence.

Since there was a shortage of everything during the war, including housing, Mom and Dad shared a small apartment with another couple, Burt and Evie. Mom worked at a local doughnut shop to augment Dad's army pay. One weekend, Dad decided to go visit his brother, Jim, who was in the Navy and recently stationed nearby. On that same weekend, Jim, knowing Dad was stationed nearby decided to visit him and his new wife, whom he had never met. And Mom had decided to visit some other friends in order to give the other couple some time to themselves.

Imagine Jim's surprise when he came to the house he had been directed to, only to find a couple on the porch and a woman sitting on the man's lap, kissing him. The man was not his brother and he wrongly assumed the woman was his new sister-in-law. Evie laughed when she told Mom how Jim's face turned beet red with confusion, anger and embarrassment. He soon recovered after hearing the facts.

But, the worm turned when Mom took him to the local P.X. for groceries. She said all the men there looked at this navy man with a 'what have we here?" look in their eyes. Mom hurriedly introduced Jim to them and explained the situation. The military must look after their own.

These letters will speak of Aunt Florence, an African-American and a very dear friend and confidant of Mom's.

"Jesse James" is a very common man's name in the south due to the hero worship of Jesse James, the outlaw. Mom had a brother, a son and her ex-spouse so named. I have tried to clarify this as I go, without losing the "spirit" of the letters.

I had always planned, with Mom's permission, to write a book about their early war experiences she had spoken of so often. She gave the letters to me to be used as I saw fit as long as I used them in an honorable way. Believe me that was no effort on my part. After reading the letters, I realized they told the story much better and more eloquently than I ever could, as their story threads its way throughout the letters. Upon transcribing the letters verbatim, I read nothing that could be considered not honorable in my estimation.

This work is another side of the W.W.II. It does not have the fighting heroes, we are accustomed to reading about or watch on the big screen. For the most part, Dad was a cook in the army and at first, not a particularly dedicated one He lost his stripes more than once. Mom has been known to have said that Velcro would have been a handy thing to have back then.

But he began to realize that an army truly does 'travel on it's stomach' and that he was a foot soldier as much as anyone. His company was somewhat like the television show, "Mash."

This is their own story of how two ordinary people meet, fall in love and strive towards fulfilling their dream of what they presume would be an extraordinary life together.

I have kept the words, grammar and all as Dad wrote them in

order to keep the essence of the man true. I have also included some negative aspect of the politics and sentiments of the day. They are not meant to offend. The reader must remember that Dad was limited in what events he could write about. I was sorry to transcribe the last letter. I wanted to see how it ended, after all was said and done.

End of Introduction

BOOK ONE

The Courting

Prologue

The greyhound bus lumbered into the station in Nashville, Tennessee. A young woman holding the hand of a tow headed five-year-old boy, climbed the steep steps and reached back to pick the boy up. He exclaimed, "I don't need no help, Mother"! The bus was nearly full and they had to take a seat in the back.

A soldier, on furlough and headed for Ohio to see his folks, stepped up into another bus; only to be informed by the driver that it was full and no seats were left. He suggested that he either get on the bus parked behind him or wait for another one that would be along in about an hour. As he climbed the steps of the next bus, it looked as if that one might be full, also. But the driver informed him there was a seat or two left in the rear. He wavered a moment, wondering whether to get on this bus or wait for one less crowded, where he could perhaps get a better seat for the long ride home. He decided to stay on this bus and thus unknowingly sealed his fate.

He worked his way to the back of the bus, attempting to avoid the feet of people already seated. He tripped over somebody's bag in the isle, lost his balance and accidentally stepped on the tow headed boy's foot, who let out a huge "squall". (Southernese for cry.) The soldier became flustered and embarrassed at hurting him and apologized profusely to the boy and his mother. He sat down beside them and engaged the child in an apologetic conversation; during which the boy declared to the soldier that his mother was divorced and not married anymore.

Being a soldier, always on the prowl and since it was a long ride to Ohio, company would be nice and female company at that. The woman and he began to exchange friendly information. Interest between them grew in leaps and bounds.

The bus neared Orlinda, Tennessee, where Mom's folks lived. She told him that this was where she must get off. Dad was smittened and wanted to know more about this woman and asked her if she thought her folks would mind if he got off with her and spend a day or two with them. There were no hotels in this small town and even if there had been, he had no money for one.

Well the South is known for its hospitality, especially in wartime. She answered that as long as he behaved himself, she didn't think they would mind

Thus, her fate was sealed.

End of Prologue

1941

Dear Cora Mae,

Well, I am in Chicago, waiting for my train. I am okay and hope this finds you the same, too. I can say I have just spent the most wonderful furlough with you. I never will forget it. I will be glad when this war is over. It will mean a lot to us.

So for now, I will close.

Dear as always, I love you,

Charles

November, 1941

Dear Cora Mae,

I got your letter and was glad to hear from you. I was late getting it as I was on maneuvers in South Carolina. Honey, I will never be able to forget you. I meant every word I said to you. If I don't mean it, I don't say it. I don't like liars. If I can't say something without lying, I don't say anything.

I am looking forward to coming to Nashville when I get back, to spend a weekend with you. We have been so busy that I did not have time to write. I sure enjoyed the time I spent with you. I would give a year of my life just to be with you again. I ought to be back in Tennessee at my camp in December I think. If this letter doesn't happen to reach you, I will write again once I am back in camp.

I guess that is all for now. I ain't got no mind for better letter writing.

Love & Best Wishes,

Charles Ward

1941

Dearest Cora Mae,

Well Honey, I haven't written you for some time because I have been pretty busy. You know how it is. Things are about the same here. No news, no excitement, no nothing. I hope this finds you all okay.

I still work in the kitchen and probably will for some time, yet. You will have to forgive me for not writing sooner, but I was too busy. When you are cooking for a hundred and fifty men, it ain't no joke.

Say hello to your folks for me and I hope you are not so blue when you get this, as you say you usually are. You know, Honey, in the army you cannot do, as you would like to. I've only been away from camp for about three times since I have been here. So you see, it ain't much fun being here.

Well, Honey, there ain't much to write about so I will close. I love you . . . do you believe me? There isn't anything in this troubled world I want more than you. Do you believe me?

Love & Best Wishes,

C.W.Ward SWAK

1941

To My Dearest Cora Mae,

Well, I wrote you a letter the other day, but I didn't have any stamps and then I naturally forgot to mail it. So I will write some more and mail them both together. I usually don't have that much to say anyway, as nothing much happens around here anyway.

I got your card but didn't get the letter you said you wrote. Honey, I am sure down hearted tonight. I sure could use some cheering up. There is nothing to do but sit around and wait I guess. I wish everyday that every Jap and German would drop dead.

Honey, why don't you write me more often? That sure would cheer me up. I know I ain't much at writing, but I don't have much time. But you could overlook that and write anyhow. I baked a cake today. It ain't so bad but it could be better. Practice makes perfect. I'll get better, sometime. Can you bake?

Well, Honey, I will close and hope to hear from you soon. I love you true.

Yours, until the kittens have cats, the cows have chickens and the chickens have kids.

I Love You, Charles

1941

My Dearest Cora Mae,

Well, Honey, I got time so I will try to make amends for being so slack in writing, henceforth. Everyday, I look for a letter from you. Everything is OK here and I hope it is there, too.

You know, we have just completed our desert maneuvers and it was the toughest six weeks I ever had the misfortune to go through. Lots of times, we had no water and a few times, very little to eat. I guess they had it planned that way, just to see if we could do it. Nobody died of it, so I guess it was a good thing just to give us an idea of what it could be like.

I don't know about my furlough, yet. I still keep hoping strong. I hope you are as anxious to see me, as I am to see you. You know now that I am out of the kitchen, I have more time to write. I hope you can read it.

Honey, are you at home now or still in Nashville, if it is any of my business? My folks are just a little slack in writing, so I don't know how they are right now. My father is getting up in years, but he still works the farm all the time. How are your folks? Getting along as well, I hope.

Let me know what you have been doing the last month or so. I can't think of too much to say, just now. I am on guard tonight, so I will have to close for now. Have all to keep hoping for me. I promise with all my might to see you soon. Please believe me.

Yours Only,

C.W.Ward Love&Kisses

1941

Dear Cora,

I got your letter when we got back from camp. We came in last night and tonight I am answering your letter. It is too bad about your brother. I hope he is okay and not hurt much. What spooked the horse?

Excuse my downhill slant. Honey, you know I would write more often, but when you are out on maneuvers, it is hard to keep track of your clothes, let alone carry along stationery.

Honey, I hope you didn't mean it when you said you were about ready to give me up. I would not have said what I did if I had not meant it. You said I would take time off to write you if I cared about you. When I get to Nashville, you will get a spanking for thinking that and I mean it.

I will tell you everything when I get there, this week or next, I don't know. I can't say as that is for my sergeant to say. It will be one or the other. But if something happens, I will let you know. I would send a picture of myself, only I don't have any. I lost all my pictures on maneuvers, even the one of you. And I also lost that address of yours, so it was a good thing I got your letter when I did.

Well, Honey, I will close for now. I don't know whether I will get off Christmas or not. If I do, you know what our plans are. Or have you given up all hope?

I will see you soon. Write to me.

Yours Only,

C.W.Ward

Roses love sunshine
Violets love dew
Angels in heaven
Know I love Yoooou!!

Excuse my scribbling. I'll write more next time.

1941
Dearest Cora Mae,

Well, Honey, I spent a nice weekend in Nashville. It would have been much more pleasant if I could have found you. I suppose you know by now, the U.S. is at war. If it goes on, you know I won't get out. But I don't worry, because I don't care how it goes but I'd rather be out. I just ain't that lucky.

You know, when I called out there at the house, I told the lady I was your boyfriend. She asked me, "which one"? What do you think of that? Haha! Don't get me wrong, cause I don't blame you. But it just sounded a little funny, that's all. She said you were at the Grand Ole' Opry.

I don't know when I will be able to get back to Nashville. Do you want me to come? I got ten days furlough sometime soon. Do you want me to figure on spending it with you? You know I meant every word I said to you. I hope you don't think of me as just someone to pass the time with. Honey, I was serious with you and I hope you were, too. You were probably angry that I didn't write sooner than I did.

Well, Honey, I only wrote home every once in awhile while I was on maneuvers and you. I am not very good at letter writing. I am just too lazy, I guess. Answer and let me know how you are and if you still want to get married. You know if we do, you will still probably doubt me.

But wait until I get my furlough . . . that is if you are still willing. You know when you are in the army, you can only do things when you get a chance. Things look pretty bad for us guys in the army, now. But I always got hope.

Tell your folks when you write to them, I said hello. I got some pictures taken the other day. I will send you some and my folks too.

Honey, please answer this letter soon as it ain't no telling what will happen next. Let me know how you feel, because it is constantly on my mind.

Yours Forever,

C.W.Ward SWAK

1941

Dearest Cora Mae,

I received your letter today. Sure was glad to get it. You know I am sorry I didn't get to see you at the bus depot. I overslept and didn't get there when I said I would. I got there at nine o'clock. I didn't get to bed very early as I did some running around in Nashville before going to bed.

The war situation is bad now, so I can't say for sure about my leave. Or even a weekend off. But we will probably get a ten day furlough soon. Half the boys will get it early and the rest of us will get it when they get back. That is if something don't happen and we get called anyway. So I will come up to see you the very first chance I get.

I hope you enjoyed the Grand Ole' Opry. I would have liked to have gone with you, but no such luck, I guess.

Everything here is as perusual. How are your brothers getting along? If you can't read this, maybe you can do some guessing.

Well I've got to close, take a shower and go to bed. So be good and answer soon.

Yours, Charles

P.S. Did you get my letter?

1941

Dearest Cora Mae,

Well, Honey, it has been awhile since I have heard from you or wrote to you. I wrote to you last week. I hope you got my letter. I don't want you to get angry because I don't write very often, but I just don't always get time. You probably think I am lying to you, but Honey, I don't lie to you. Why should I? I don't want you to stop writing because I don't write often enough.

What are you doing these days? We had a parade today. Boy, I hate those. They are taking our horses away and mechanizing us. I don't like the idea, but what can I do?

How are things doing in Tennessee anyway? How are the crops? I wonder often of how you are doing. I sure miss getting your letters because I look forward to getting them. You said you would always love me no matter what. Do you still mean that? I hope you do.

I can't think of much to say, except I would like to be there with you. So I will say so long for now and ask you to write to me soon.

Love, Charles SWAK

P.S. Honey, please believe me. You are the one who can make me unhappy if you didn't love me. I hope this damn war ends soon.

Honey, please believe me when I say I love you, because I really mean it and I want you to believe that, too. Well, so long again. Write very soon.

1941

Dearest Cora Mae,

Well, I wasn't going to write you today, but I got your letter with the picture in it, so I thought I would write and thank you. You said it wasn't a very good picture, but you know you are mistaken. In my mind, I think you are, anyway. It is a very good picture. I sent a couple of pictures of me earlier. You should get them soon, if not already.

I am trusting in you a lot so don't let me down. I have always told you the truth except when I am joking with you and I want you to do the same. Don't get mad if I say something when I am teasing you or joking with you. Let me know if you do so I can correct it, Okay? And you do the same, will you? I don't believe in joking when one is trying to be serious. So be serious with me. Will you?

You said in your letter that you get lonesome. Well, I don't get lonesome, but I do get homesick to see you.

Well, there isn't much more to write about, but I do want to thank you for your picture.

Write back. From one who loves you, Charles SWAK

1941

Dearest Cora Mae,

Well, Honey, I sure hope you are still in Tennessee when you get this. I am OK and hope this finds you the same. Everything here is okay. Is it there?

We are figuring on a ten-day furlough, but I don't think I will be able to get home in that length of time. It is twenty-six hundred miles and that is quite a ways.

I hope you love me as I do you. How is everyone? Are you still at home? I would like to get enough time to come and see you. But, no use hoping for it. I sure will be glad when this war ends. I would like to kill every Jap on earth and then we would never be bothered again.

How are the crops in Tennessee? Everything here is the same and I hope it stays that way.

I've got to get ready for retreat, so I've got to hurry some. Please remember this, I love you and always will; no matter where I am and what happens. I sure get lonesome out here. I could use some time in your company. I guess that would help me a lot. Darling, you don't know what I would give to be with you or near you. So don't forget, I love you and always will.

Please answer soon. Tell all I said hello.

Yours, Charles SWAK I Love You

1941

Dear Cora Mae,

It has been quite a while since I wrote you. We have been out on patrol and since we got back, they have really kept us busy. I haven't got a letter for sometime, but I guess if a person doesn't write, then he doesn't get any.

You probably gave up on me by now, but you said you would always be mine. If I can depend on that, I still love you as always.

The government lets us send our mail free now. There are rumors going around that I can't discuss in the mail, but it looks favorably for our outfit in the near future. I hope you will forgive me for my long speech in not writing. But we have been busy. I hope you don't wait as long.

How is everybody back there? Fine I hope. I am still cooking, but I am getting pretty damn tired of it. Well, Honey, if things let up, I will write you more often. Remember me as the one who loves you best of all and keep y our chin up high.

C.W.Ward

P.S. Sending all my love and best wishes. SWAK

1941

Dearest Cora Mae,

Well Dear, I received your letter and was glad to get it. I sure enjoy hearing from you.

We get a ten day furlough and I sure would like to come and see you. But, I don't think there is time to get there and back. And I don't have the necessary money to make my trip there and back, so I am afraid I will not be able to come and see you.

Honey, you will never know how much I long to see you. It seems like years since I last saw your sunny smile on your pretty face. If I could only find some way or a kind hearted person who could find their way to loan me the money, then I would come to see you.

Now Darling, if I am able to come and see you, do you think it would be possible for us to be together and alone?? Sweetheart, you know when I was there last with you, what I had in mind and what terms we got acquainted. Now if this is asking too much, let me know and then I will go home where I know I can get what I want. You know what I want and why it is. You know, when you are in the army, you never know how long you are going to be around. So I figure, I better do while the doing is good.

Don't forget, I will always love you, no matter what. Now, don't get angry over this letter. If you don't agree, it is no sign I don't love you or you don't love me.

Honey, I really don't like to write like this, but you have had more experience than me, so you should understand better than most girls. That is why I ask this. You will probably think I don't love you, but do you think I would spend my only leave I may ever have again, just to be with you? Over everything else, down deep in my heart I truly love you. And if you truly love me, you will want to make me happy, as I know you can and you should be willing to make this sacrifice for me. I know I would do anything to see and be near you. I don't think it is asking too much. Honey, I want your honest answer, so answer this letter soon, as time is short.

Please, Darling, don't get mad and stop writing, as it would break my heart not to get a letter from you. You probably think I am a fool for writing this but I just can't help it.

Well, Honey, please try to agree with this. I hope you will try to understand how it is.

But, Darling, I love you and hope to hear from you and willing to be with you soon. A million hugs and kisses for my little missus.

Bye, Honey

Author's note, (Turkey!!)

1941
To The One I Love,

Hello Darling,

Well another day has gone by and I am glad of it. It brings me one more day closer to you. I hope so anyway. How are you doing? We have nonclemature of our rifles today. It is getting interesting. Hope you have gotten my letters as I sent them airmail. I hope the answer is on its way here.

How did the crops come out? I guess my folk's crops did good this year. Dad was sure tickled, anyway. We should know about our furlough soon. As soon as I find out, I will let you know.

It is about time for us to stand retreat now, so I must close. It is about suppertime here and that is the best part of the day. Mealtime. Haha If and when I get my furlough, oh boy, Tennessee, here I come!

Well retreat is over. I stood three hours. They showed a movie tonight, but I didn't go as I didn't seem to have no interest in it. The time sure drags along. It seems like ages since I last saw you. I hope you will be home when I get there. I am laying on my cot, writing this. We sleep in a tent, six fellows to a tent. It is a nice arrangement. But not as nice when compared to Camp Forrest in Tennessee or Camp Ord. in Oklahoma.

Well, Darling, I must close,

Pvt. Ward, San Diego, California SWAK

P.S. Excuse my writing as I am in a hurry, but want to add a few more lines. You know, Honey, about us getting married: how long does it take and how long I spend there depends on how fast our train connections are scheduled. I don't know, also, about the money I will have left when I get there.

How much will it cost for us to get married and how long does it take. Let me know so I can plan things out. I want to marry you if I possible can, on this furlough. I haven't had a chance to see about my train ticket, yet.

So you see, the only thing I can't say anything with certainty, except I love you. I am a no good, but if you say you love me and if I can marry you, then it will be your bad mistake. What do you think?

So until I write again, I'll say so long,

Charles W. Ward SWAK

1941

Well, Darling,

Another day has passed and all is well, including myself.

Honey, I got your letter today and was proud to hear from you. I reckon by now you have got my letter. You are probably madder than a hornet. But time heals all wounds, they tell me. I hope you are not angry with me, as it would break my heart.

I've been looking for an answer from you everyday. I guess I am just too anxious. Yet it will probably be no. But yet, before my furlough I will have lots of time to write. Maybe you will hate me for writing a letter like that. I hope not.

How are you at picking blackberries by now? They promoted me to first cook after all. What do you think of that!? I get a little more pay and a lot less work. Maybe I will turn out to be a pretty good cook after all.

Will you send another picture of yourself? I lost the ones that I had on maneuvers. I sure would like another one very much. Well Darling, keep this in mind, I love you and always will. Do you think deep in your heart, you love me as you say? Please write to me soon, as I like to get your letters. And I do want to see you very much.

I can't think of much else to say only that I hope things go right so I can see you. I leave it up to you, one way or the other. Just be true as you once promised and I will be okay.

Yours Forever & Then Some,

C.W.Ward I Love You

1941

Dearest Cora Mae,

Well, I ain't received any answer from you yet, so I thought I would write and see if you were dead. Did you get my last letter? If you did, why don't you write me? Or don't you care to. Why can't we be friends like we could be? We are no different now than we were then. Maybe someday, we will be glad we are friends.

How are things going for you now? Are you working or not? Let me know, if it isn't any of my business.

Well, I can't think of much more to say just now. If I don't get any letters from you, I will just have to drop it, I guess. If you do write, let me know how you are doing and how you are getting along.

Well, that is all for now, Honey. Please write me a letter.

Yours Forever & Then Some,

Charles W. Ward SWAK

1941

To The One I Love,
Dearest Cora Mae,

Well. Darling, I suppose you gave up on me by now. I told you I was a funny kind of guy. I just got a lazy spell and didn't write. I went home for my furlough as my father said I should, as I might never have gotten a chance to go again.

Things have been pretty good for me the last couple of months. I am a sergeant now but I am still a cook.

Honey, I hope you will answer this letter and hope you have not found anybody else to love, yet. I still love you and always will, even though I might act like I don't. We are out on the Mohave Desert now, on maneuvers. Boy the sun sure is hot. We are suppose to go to Fort Org, sometime soon. Now don't be surprised if you don't hear from me for a while. We don't get much time to write many letters when we are on these maneuvers

If you are mad at me, I can't help it now. But when I get out of the army, I am coming to Tennessee to marry my girl anyhow, if she would answer and let me know if she is mad at me. I hope she isn't mad at me for going home on my furlough. But if I would have come to see you, we would have been married and in a couple of days I would have had to leave you and I don't want that. If I get married, I want to be free, so I can stay with my wife. Write and let me know how you feel about me. Every time I think of being married, I think of what I would do with a wife. I wonder if I would be able to support her. That seems to scare me and I lose faith in myself.

Honey, that is the big reason I didn't write you for so long. I guess I am afraid of taking on the responsibility of having a wife. I don't think anyone wants a wife more than me, but I just can't bring myself to do it. I don't know whether I am afraid or what. I can go so far on the idea of marrying and then I want to get away from it. I can't explain but maybe you can get a general idea.

You once said I was different from most boys. I guess you were right. I like women and sex and most every other thing about them. But having one depending on me to look out for just seems to scare me or something. It is true, I would like to have you out here as my wife. But, Honey, I don't want to bring you out here. I don't know why. What do you think I ought to do? Write to me soon.

Well, I must get ready to wash up and get supper. Please don't get mad at me and answer soon. My address is on the envelope of the letter I last sent you.

From the One Who Loves You and Wants You, Please write soon.

Bye Darling SWAK Love& Kisses

December 21, 1941

Dear Cora Mae,

Well, Kid, I will write you again and hope you will think enough of me to read my letter. I suppose by now, I have lost clear out with you. Well, all I can say is this, I am sorry. But I have lost before so that is nothing new to me. I received your last letter and got sore, so I didn't answer.

I never was one to love and leave as I thought I would do when I met you on the bus. I surely am sorry of it now, as I know I was wrong. So, Honey, I sincerely hope you and your boyfriend are happy now. That is more than I can say for myself just now. But time cures all. I just want one more letter from you just to know how you are getting along. If you want, we will both go our own way. I won't hang onto a woman, no matter how much she means to me.

I am a full blooded Englishman. I am just as hard headed as an Englishman. My ways are mine, yours is yours and I can't change either of them. If you love me as you say you did, it wouldn't matter if I wrote often, as long as I wrote. But, if nothing happens, it is out for us. I will say I will never forget you or quit loving you, but I will get along without you.

So send me one more letter. I will be looking for it. Send it to me at my old address at Fort Ord, as we are moving back there now.

From the one who loves you and will always be your friend. I hope we meet again under better circumstances.

Love, Charles

1941

Dearest Cora Mae,

I got your letter and sure was glad to hear from you. Well, I thought you had got mad at me and wasn't going to write anymore. That would have been a bad thing to happen to me just now, because my spirit is sure getting low, being so far away from the one you love.

If I ever get out of the army, I am coming straight to Tennessee because that is where my heart longs to be.

I got a letter from an old girlfriend, the one you asked me about. She wants me to start writing her again, but I won't because it takes up too much of my time from writing to you. Besides, as long as I am getting letters from you, I have no desire to write to her. She must have asked my folks for my address because I haven't written to her since I met and started writing to you.

(Fragment of a letter)

January 1942

Dearest Cora Mae,

I received your ever-welcomed letter today.

Honey, if you think I blame a married woman for having three children makes any diff to me, you are all wet! You also said you wouldn't blame me if I didn't write or want to hear from you. In other words, it sounds as if you are trying to get rid of me and my correspondence.

Honey, if that is your idea, then say so plainly and if it ain't, quit writing like that. I don't like to say it like that, but I have told you several times that your past is of no concern of mine and I want it forgotten. I will not say anything about it to you or anybody else. So you remember this, YOU are loved, not your past. I don't like for you to get mad because that would hurt me. You know I only want you to know my feelings toward you.

I sure hope what Jr. said comes true. I am sorry if things don't come out well for you at home. I sure wish I could be there with you. Every once in awhile, I think of you and those stars we looked at. So, remember, I LOVE YOU! So think of that.

Answer soon. Say hello to your folks.

Loving you always,

Charles

January 1942

My Dearest Cora Mae,

You probably don't know what to think. Here you got three letters in a row, at least from me.

I might as well tell you, they put me in the hospital yesterday. I wasn't going to tell you, but it is through no fault of my own that I am here. Of that I am most sure. It is for the itch. There is quite a lot of it out here and I was just lucky enough to get a handful or two of it. You probably think I am full of hooey, but think as you might, I can't lie about it.

I sure wish I was in Tennessee. You know I told these fellows that I would walk out of here with both legs broken, if they would give me a discharge. But they wouldn't listen. Haha. That is how bad I want to get back to you. I just don't have the words to tell you how I feel about you. If I was near, I would probably want to show you. Haha. But then I would probably do a poor job because I ain't much at love making.

Well, Honey, I had better sign off, now. Write to me. You said something once about there is going to be two whippings. Well, I know there will be one, at least.

Well, Honey, I will close for now. Don't forget me.

I love you, forever and ever.

Charles W. Ward

1942

Dearest Cora Mae,

Well, Honey, I've got awhile before they turn out the lights. I am still getting treated. I am okay but I didn't get any better today. I didn't get a letter from you today, so you have a paddling coming. I know you don't think I could paddle you, but I have my own ideas on that.

If I ever get out of here, I will not even join church. Joining the army sure broke me of joining anything, here on out. Haha Honey, I wish you would write so I would have questions to answer. I can't think of anything to write about.

Are you still keeping house for that woman in Nashville? I get to thinking and wondering what you are doing. Let me know. Is your ex-husband still around or has he forgotten you? Does he come around? Does he make you any trouble?

Honey, I hope this war blows over soon so we can see each other again. If the Russians and McArthur keep it up, it looks like they won't have to be fighting long. I hope so anyway.

Sweetheart, that is all for now. I am all out of words. I will write some more tomorrow.

Please Answer Soon,

Charles Ward

1942

Dearest Cora Mae,

Well, I am out of the hospital now. I got your present and was very glad to get it. I want to thank you. It was the only one I got, as my folks don't believe too much in giving presents. I will send yours as soon as I can. I haven't any money right now. I will get paid in a few days.

Well, as usual, there ain't much to say, as there ain't no news. It is about time for lights to go out, so I must close,

I want to thank you again for your thoughtfulness.

Remaining Yours,

C.W.Ward

Love & Best Regards Answer soon SWAK

1942

Well, Honey, I got three letters from you today. That tinted picture of you sure looks nice.

I got out of the hospital a week ago. I went to the dentist this morning and had to have a tooth removed. I got to go back next week to get two more pulled. They are growing so I figure, just let the army do it, as it doesn't cost me anything.

Excuse the downhill slant. I am in bed writing this and I am also left handed.

I think you are doing best by going back home. Your folks and children need you there. But if things get too tough, you use your better judgment. You probably think I've got my nerve telling you what to do.

Honey, if you think your letters might make me stop loving you, you are off track.

Well, I must close and pack my locker as we are going on a march tomorrow. I hope this letter finds you.

Love & Best Wishes, Charles W. Ward

1942

To My Dear and Sweet Cora Mae,

I got your letter today and was glad and surprised when you did write. I began to think you were not going to write me anymore. Things are still the same, no news or anything and nothing to do.

You say you wish I could be there. Honey, you don't wish it anymore than I do. You asked if I remembered the place where we got engaged and sat and watched those stars. I will never forget those things and I wish things had gone the way we wanted it to then. Honey, I have a constant longing in my heart for you and I sure wish you were here with me. Do you wish I were there? That is my idea of heaven.

A few of the boys have their women here. I don't know how they do it in order to keep them here. You know some of the boys are being transferred to the military police. I would like that as I would not have to leave the states. But I just ain't that lucky.

Honey, I can't think of much else to say except I love you. I hope I hear from you soon and often.

Love & Best Wishes, I TRUULY LOOOOVE YOOOU!!,

Charles W. Ward

1942

To my dearest, dearest Cora Mae,

Well, Honey, I got your letter yesterday and was glad to hear you were okay. You are probably going to be mad at me when you get this letter because I have not written sooner. I have been busy though.

You know, Honey, if things go right, maybe you can come out here to see me or even stay, if I can keep you. You know I get sixty-one dollars per month, if they give us the ten dollar raise like they said they will. Do you think you can get along on that much? I will have to have expense money, too. I don't know how much it will cost for you to get out here. It might be worth a try, though.

Well, I got to get ready for retreat now. I will finish this afterward.

Well, retreat is over, so I will finish this. I am sorry for not writing sooner. I am just lazy, I guess. I hope you will forgive me. There is something going on now, that is not to be discussed here or anywhere else. You know how that is. I got a letter from my brother the other day and he is getting closer to going into the army every day now. The army wouldn't hurt him any, I don't think. He has always been footloose, anyhow. Of course I don't wish any bad luck for him such having to work in the kitchen. It sure gets tiresome in there.

Well, I can't think much else to say. I hope this finds you well and okay. How are your folks anyhow? Hope they are well. I guess you will be sore by the time when you get this. I promise I will be more prompt next time.

Yours forever,

Charles Ward

I LOVE YOOOOU!! SWAK

Dearest Cora Mae,

I got your letter today and boy was I glad to get it. I also got your present. I wrote you a letter earlier, telling you so. Maybe you didn't get it. We are going to move, but not too far, I don't think. I will let you know if we do.

I got confined for a week for going to a show without a pass. Honey, I will send you a present as soon as I can get to town to get it. Ain't got much at camp to sell for a woman. I don't know what it will be. I don't know much about selecting for a woman. Honey, you can stop worrying about me letting you down, because I never will. That is a promise you can hold me to my dying day. I sure wish I could be there today and forever.

Things are sure dead here now. Nothing to see . . . nothing to do. I wish they would move us back to Tennessee, but I don't think miracles like that will happen. Do you? But, with God's help. I will get back to you some way.

You can write my folks if you want. Here is their address. They might be a little slow in answering back. They are slow answering my letters, too. Honey, you sound as if you are worried about my folks liking you. If things should happen to be that way, it would make no diff to me, because, I am the one you need to make like you. But, I don't think they will care. They never did as long as I liked them.

I don't think I will go back to Ohio, anyway. I figure on changing my life a little when I get back to you.

Well, Honey, I need to stop writing for now and go to bed. I have to get up at three in the morning to help get breakfast for the men. Did I tell you I was an army cook? Not a very good one, I can tell you. But I don't do the main cooking. I peel potatoes and vegetables and scrub the pans.

I will write to you tomorrow, as I will be off.

Love & best wishes,

Your faithful Charles SWAK

1942

Dearest Cora Mae,

You can't know how surprised I was to hear from you. I really thought you would forget me. I am glad you didn't though.

You said you had been busy with the crops. I sure hope they did good for your folks. Well, I have been busy, too. We went on a three-day bivouac and we sure had a time. We are a mechanized force now. I am first cook now and hold a sergeant technician rating. I get seventy-eight dollars a month. Not bad, huh?

I could have you come out here to stay, but living expenses are high. I might get you out here and then would not be able to help you. What would you do then? Honey, You know, as I said before, nothing would make me happier than to have you out here with me. But, then, I always think to myself, what if I got you out here and lost my rating? Or what if I had to go away?

Also, Honey, it is like this. I get seventy-eight dollars a month. I don't know whether I can keep you on that or not. But because, now that I know you are not mad at me, if you want to come out and see how things are, I will see to it that you come out. But, it will be two or three months, as we are going on a three month maneuver. But, as soon as I get back, I will send for you. I will do all I can to keep you out here. But if things don't work out, I won't stand for any nagging, or any other wrongdoing. If you really love me, it won't be hard on us, I don't think. Now, Honey, think it over careful. I will close for now and wait for your answer.

Honey, your letter made me the happiest boy in the world, because now I know you ain't mad at me.

Hoping to see you soon and loving you forever and always. Please believe me when I say that I love you. SWAK . . . Please answer soon.

I am going to try to get my furlough in the next ten days or sooner. And if I do, I should see you within fifteen days or so. When you see me, don't be surprised if I am a different color. I am more white now, as I have been doing inside work.

Truly Yours, C.W.Ward SWAK

To The Sweetest Girl I Ever Knew,
Cora Mae, I Love You,

I received your letter last evening so I am answering it now. We were suppose to get our mess sergeants diploma. But I was on duty and forgot to go. I will probably get a bawling out, but I am use to those guys by now. I guess my mind ain't on my work. You probably know where my mind is.

About you getting your hair cut off. You can have it cut, but don't cut it too short. I liked the way it was. But I can imagine how it must feel in the hot weather. You can cut it but don't do what I did. Mine is about one-fourth inch all over. When we work in the kitchen, they want our hair short for sanitary reasons.

You know, I think the reason my folks don't write me more often is that they are too busy. Anyhow, they could write once in awhile. I hope I can always make your folks respect me. All I can say is that I will always try to do the right thing for them. I don't know about me being the head of you and the business. I don't think that is necessary. They always say two heads are better than one, so we had better put both our heads together and use it as one. We will always be better satisfied that way.

I long to be with you to give you a good loving. But we have to wait, I guess. But maybe not for too long, I hope. It ain't long before I will be entitled to another fifteen days according to army rules. I just hope I get it when the time comes

Well. Honey, I had better sign off now. I want to write my folks, so I'd better get busy.

Just remember, I adore you, I love you, I worship you.

Yours Forever, Charles

To the one and only rose in my heart. (Two hearts with their initials and an arrow connecting them.)

P.S. You can look for me within fifteen days as I just got word that my furlough is official. We can straighten things out then. SWAK

Dearest Darling, Cora Mae,

Yes, darling, I miss you, too, but I won't be able to see you very often, as we are so far apart. The only thing I can say is just wait and see. That may be a long time. You said something about having the flu. It is so hard to think of it being flu season as it is so warm and sunny out here. It is just like summer. I sure hope you will be okay though. If I had the money, I would have you out here with me, just soaking up the sun. That would have to do you some good.

Honey, I hope you are not doing wrong by working in Nashville. You know your mother asked me to try to get you to come home. But I figured you are old enough to do what is best for you. I just want you to be careful and good.

Please remember to look at those stars as we did when I was there. I can never forget that night in Tennessee with you. I will say now, that I almost didn't get on that bus, but I am glad I did, because now, I have something to look forward to. If you had been the other way, I would have figured you just another girl. So, believe me when I say I love you.

I had a couple of pictures taken to send you last week. You can probably tell I was half shot. But don't worry, I only get that way every few months and then only to drown my memories. I promise not to drink too much and if you have any feelings against it, why I will quit altogether. But while I am in the army, I don't think it hurt very much. What do you think? But that is all a person can do around here. You don't have to worry about me being a drunkard or anything, because I don't drink that well.

Well. Cora Mae, I need to sign off for now as it is chow time. That is the only good thing around here.

Remember, I love you. Charles SWAK

1942

Dearest Cora Mae,

Well, Honey, I ain't got nothing else to do so I thought I would write you a few lines. Everything her is as usual. Hope the children are okay. What are you doing now? Are you still at the same place or not? You know you've got to watch out for the good of yourself and don't do anything you might be sorry of. The idea of you alone in a town like Nashville is not to my liking. But, of course, you surely ought to know what is best for you. I just wish I could be there to watch out for you.

Honey, I don't know why I fell so hard for you. Don't forget that picture of you as I really want it. What does your folks think of me anyhow? Do they ever say? What do they think of us getting married when I get back there?

I sure wish I were there now. I hope to hear from you soon. From one who loves you best. Here's to your and my luck. I hope it is not too long. I don't think Japan is big enough to bother the USA.

Does your ex ever bother you when you are in Nashville? Do you ever think of going back to him? I hope not, but if you do I won't stop you. But it is truly my belief that you would be making a terrible mistake. But it is up to you.

Take a picture of you and the three children together and send it to me. I sure want to have one. But you can do that when you have more time on your hands.

Well, Darling, I must close for now. Please remember I love you with all my heart.

Charles

Sept. 1942

Dearest Cora Mae,

Got your letter today and I was sure glad to get it. I look for a letter everyday. I guess I expect too much, but I sure enjoy reading them. I think that woman who told you I was a good boy has me judged wrong. Or don't I think much of myself? Or do I?

Honey, I told you once that your past life would be forgotten when we are together forever and always. Look at it this way . . . the past is the past. The future is still to be. My past has been no bed of roses, so we are just about even, as far as I can see. And if you love me and I love you, I can't see that it is anybody's business, but our own. Anything that has happened in the past ought to be forgotten. But, Honey, use your own judgment on what you do and the way you want to do. And if you are still there for me when I get back, we will do what we should have done when we first met, instead of waiting.

Do your folks know we intend to marry? What did they say? What did they think? Honey, I don't like to say anything, but if your ex-husband still wants to marry you again and you want to, please do as your heart tells you. There isn't anything in this world more priceless than happiness. And after all, you should know what your heart wants. I am still in love with you and always will be. Nothing can change that and never will.

You know I never tell anyone something I don't mean. I told you I love you, so what more can I do? You will probably doubt me. I don't blame you. If we both live right, everything will come out if you decide to go back with your ex-husband. I couldn't if I wanted to.

I can't think of much more to say. Please believe me when I tell you that you are the only one that I love. I read your letters and wonder what to write about after I answered your letters, so I will close. Please don't doubt my love for you. Write to me often.

Charles W. Ward I love you.

Dearest Cora Mae,

Well, Honey, I didn't get to write you yesterday afternoon as I had promised in my last letter. But, now is just as well. My confinement will be lifted Saturday if I don't get into any more trouble.

Yesterday, we all had to pack out bags as though we were going to move out. We went out on an all day ride and then came back and unpacked out bags. Some joke!!! I guess it was just for practice.

Hope you are not as blue when you get this letter as I am now. You ought to be more happy now that you are near your children. I don't remember whether I sent you my folk's address or not, so I will include it in this letter. If you write to them, send me their answer, as I would like to know how they feel, one way or the other. It makes no diff between you and me as far as I am concerned.

How are your folks? Okay I hope.

Honey, I would like your viewpoint on what we are going to do when I get out of here. I am best adapted to farm life as it has always been mostly what I have done. What about you? I can cook but never would be a very good chef. My heart isn't in it. I have never worked in a factory in my life. What do you think? What is your honest opinion? Tell me in your answer to this.

Everyone is quiet now. It is time for lights out. So will close.

Darling, I love you, C.W. Ward

You asked me if I remember the stars at night and the window you crawled through. I remember that night as though it happened just last night. I remember those stars every night when we were sitting on the road, whenever I think of you.

1942

To the woman I love until I die.
Cora Mae, I Love You,

Well, a few lines to catch you up on things. I pray this finds you well. I would not like to think of you in any other way. I am going to the hospital tomorrow to take an examination for working in the kitchen. We've got to take them ever so often. I will send you your gift toward the first or last of this month or the next as that is when we get paid.

Honey, do you want to save money for us to start on? If so, I will send you part of my pay in a money order. It will be a help to us when and if I get out. And if I don't, then it will be yours. Then I know when I get out, I will know you are still my own. Let me know so I will know what to do. Honey, you are the only thing I got left, so don't let me down. It might get my Irish up.

Honey, remember the one who has put all his love to someone I have only seen once but live to see again. Say hello to your folks and the children.

Love & Best Wishes, Charles

P.S. I can't find my pictures, but I will look for them. I think they are in my other jacket that is locked up in the supply room. I will send them when I find them.

1942

Dearest Cora Mae,

Well, Honey, I guess I got time to write again. It is really getting cold here. I guess the heat is over for now. We haven't had rain for a long time. Hope we don't either because living in tents and rain don't mix.

We got our furlough, but we got to give our destination. When I told them I was going to Orlinda, Tennessee, they said if I was going to see my folks, I could go now. I would have to go later to see you and then I might not get my furlough at all. So I gave them my folk's address. I will go home and try to get down there if I can.

I would like for you to meet me in Louisville, Kentucky. The trouble is, I don't know what time I will get there, as I don't know how long it will take for me to get there. Well, I would be there one way or another, I can tell you that. You would be home and I would not fool you like I did the last time. I am very sorry about that, now. I won't do it again.

To tell you the truth, I never spent a happier day or night like the one I spent with you. You don't realize how much you love someone until you can't be with them for a year or so. It has been one year and one month since we saw one another. But it won't be long now if nothing happens to stop me.

To tell you the truth, I had to pull a fast one to get this furlough this time. Just so they don't find out until I am on my way home. So, until I see you, keep your fingers crossed and here's hoping and wish me luck.

Yours, Forever, I Love You, Charles

BOOK TWO

Newly Married

November 1942

TO MY DARLING WIFE, CORA MAE,

Well, Darling, I am in the Chicago station waiting for my train. It sure is terrible to think we are parted again. You will never know just how happy you have made me. There will never be another week in my life that will be so dear to me. I was scared at first, but now I can say I am truly proud you are my wife and I hope she is proud to have me as her husband. Honey, you can say you have done your part in this life by giving this soldier the happiness he has been looking for all of his life. There can never be anyone who can come between us in this life, now. I want you to be at ease about that. There is just one ambition in my life and that is to make you happy from now on.

Honey, please don't do anything to hurt either one of us. I never knew just how much we meant to each other until we had to part. I hope you are as happy to be my wife as I am to be your husband. I can't say in words how much you mean to me.

Tell your folks that the kindness I received while I was there was the best I have ever received anywhere. Maybe someday I can return it to them in some way.

You are the only one who has ever made me happy and I will try to do the same for you.

Your Devoted Husband, C.W. Ward

1942

To My Dearest Wife,

Well, Honey, I am back in camp now, laying on my cot, writing to you and also feeling very lonesome for you. You don't know how happy you have made me. If only we could have stayed together instead of parting.

How are the children getting along? Did Jr. like his pretty? Honey, someday we will be together and can do things together and we will become more sure of ourselves. That sure will be a happy day for us, won't it?

Honey, I would have liked very much to get that doll we were looking at in the store window in Franklin, but I was too short on money. I could tell by the way you were looking at it that you probably wanted it for one of the little girls. Was I right? Someday things will be different.

Honey, tell your folks I said hello and for them to write me once in awhile, if they would.

Well, Darling, I must close for now and go to bed. Early morning you know. So answer soon.

From one who is very happy to be your husband,

C.W.Ward SWAK

To My Dearest Wife, Cora Mae, I Love You,

Honey, I received your letter of the 21st and 22nd today. You can't imagine how glad I was to get them. Tell Bill glory for him for not passing the army. The army doesn't need him near as bad as your folks. When he gets married, wish him good luck and best wishes from me.

Honey, you don't know how hungry I get for you. But, like you say, there will be a day for us. Someday, we will be able to get our dinner anytime we are hungry. I am sure glad you are saving those passes for me. We may be apart a long time, Honey, and it will probably seem hopeless at times. But I can truly say I have had one week of the most sacred thing I can ever ask for. To me, you mean life itself. I will love you until the day I die.

Honey, if you think you did anything wrong while I was there, you are mistaken. Everything you did was okay by me. I love you for the way you treated me. You are very dear to me and I can truly say I have never loved anyone like I do you.

Memories of you will never die. Do you remember that little silk flower you gave me? I still got it. I look at it often and I think of how you looked at me when you gave it to me. I hope to still have it when I get back, if I can. I can never forget the first week of our married life. I was never so happy in my life.

Remember, I live only for you. I only want to make you happy as you made me. Only then, will our life be complete. So don't never doubt my love for you.

I Love You, Your Husband, Charles SWAK

1942

To the Dearest Girl I Know, My Wife, Cora Mae,

I just received your letter of the twenty-third. You asked why I was in such a hurry to get away from you in town that day and where

I was when you came up town to look for me. Honey, I went to the store where the bus stop was. Then I went over to the courthouse and sat on a bench until the bus came.

You asked me why I was in a hurry to leave you. Well, Honey, I don't think you are being fair to say that to me. Honey, leaving you was the hardest thing I ever had to do. I wasn't in a hurry, but I knew if I didn't leave you then, it would be a lot harder when I did, for both of us.

Please don't think I wanted to get away from you, because I didn't. It was really because I had to leave you. I kept thinking and my head was in a buzz. If I acted funny to you, I am sorry, but please don't think I didn't love you because I do. I am very happy now even if I was worried and afraid of getting married. Now I am proud I got you as my wife and will do everything I can to make you love me.

Honey, I have always told you the truth and I always will. Write and tell me if you believe what I tell you. And you do love me, don't you? Let me know. I want you to know I love and believe in you, so Honey, don't make me feel different. You are the only one in the world that can make me happy, now. I love you and I really mean it more than anything in the world and want that you believe what I say. I want you to be able to say you love me and believe it in your mind. Because I know you are the only one I will ever love.

I have folks and I have a good home and could have gone on to my furlough and wanted to very much, as I miss them. But I came to be with you, as I could never get you off my mind. Every night, I would look at those stars and remember you on the night we spent together. So I came to see you. When you came to the door, I knew then that I wanted you and I can't say why, because love is something no one can explain.

Honey, I had to love you a lot to spend my furlough with you and not go home to see my father and mother. But, Darling, I am glad I came to see you, now. So, don't ever forget I love you. I want you to believe me. You do, don't you? I don't care what anyone says or does, I will keep on loving you until you make me quit loving you. I don't want your folks to think I wanted to leave you. But, the longer I stayed with you, the harder it was to leave.

I will send you pictures as soon as I get paid. How are the boys' corn crop doing? You asked me about my drinking. I don't drink anything but water now and know you want it that way. Don't ever worry about me being a drunkard because, I won't drink if you don't want me to.

Tell your folks I said hello and good luck. I will be glad to see them again when this war is over. When I get out of here, I can prove to them and anyone else of my love for you.

They are singing, "I am Thinking Tonight of My Blue Eyes" . . . on the radio, just now. It sure makes me blue. Please write me a letter if you have any doubts about my love for you. You don't think we made a mistake, do you? I don't. Please write and let me know how you feel about our marriage. Tell me the truth and then I won't worry about your love for me anymore. That is, if you love me like I love you.

Honey, I read this letter over to myself and I can't think of much more to say that will help you to know and believe in me. Until then, I am one who will always love you. Write me soon and answer the questions. But please believe in me as that I is what I want you to do. Please don't doubt me. Send me a picture of the children.

From One Who Loves You,

Your Husband, C.W. Ward

December 19, 1942

Dearest Wife,

I started this letter last night but had mailed one yesterday and thought I would write more to this one. I have some bad news. We are moving out of here and going up to the state of Oregon. We are suppose to leave in a week or ten days. But I will be okay. That state is suppose to be awfully cold.

It will be a big change in climate. I got your letters and was glad to get them. Your letters are all that I enjoy out here and I read them over and over. I sent you a gift. I hope you like it. When you open it, get all the love and kisses I would give you if I were there. I didn't send the children any present as I am broke. When I do get my pay, I will send money and you can get them something. I sent you about ten dollars about four weeks ago. Will you say in one of your letters if you got it?

Honey, will you can get the children's birth certificates and send them to me? I need their ages, birthdays and the full name of each as I will need them for the allotment. You can send them here to me if you want and if I ain't here they will forward it to me. I know it is a lot of bother and will take time. I will do my best to get it for you and them. It will mean eighty dollars. I want you to have it. You are my wife and any soldier with a wife is entitled to it. So I think it is my job to get it for you. I know it will be a help to you and it would make me feel good to get it for you because of how happy you have made me.

If I get another furlough, I could not think of not spending it with you. That is the only place I want to be. There would be nothing better than to take you up to my folks place. I know they will like you because they like nice people and you are one of the nicest girl I know. You are the world to me. The past does not matter. Only the future counts. You are the woman I love and only God can stop me from loving you now.

I am sorry Bill has to go. But tell him to keep his chin up and it will be okay. You do believe me when I say I love you and truly believe in you, don't you? Don't ever think another woman will kiss me cause you are the only one who will, after kissing you. You are the best girl to kiss and I wish I was kissing you now.

I would sure make you holler "uncle." I would squeeze you until you turned blue. I can just feel you in my arms now. You don't know how much I want to be near you again. You might think I am kidding you when I say things like that. But when I come back to live with you, I will prove it. I will always love and be proud of you. If this is not the truth, then I would ask God to take my life right this minute. You have to do more than spank and sass me to stop me from loving you.

Did you put powder or perfume on your last letter? I can't forget holding you in my arms. I knew then I would always want your love and love is a lot stronger than fear. So, now I am glad I am married. I know no one can make me happier than you. There isn't anything I want more than to have a life together with you. Someday we will be together and we will never part again as we were meant to be together always.

I Love You,

Your husband, Charles

1942

To My Dearest Sweetest Wife, Cora Mae,

Just a few lines to say hello and to say everything here is okay.

Hope you are the same. We are pretty well set up here at our new camp. I sure miss you. I wish we were together. I got your letter with my sis's letter in it. I'm glad she wrote you. She is a good kid. She didn't day anything about the "increase" that is on the way. I hope she made it okay. She isn't very big.

Honey, have you heard anything about the allotment I made out for you? They will probably write and ask you some questions. Let me know if they do. Or, if you hear anything of it. I don't know how long it will be before you start getting any money. That is what worries me. I know it would help you and I want you to have it.

I can't get that pillowslip for your mother until they get some in the PX or army store. They should get some in soon as it is about Christmas. My folks wrote me the other day. I guess they have decided not to get mad at us. I am glad. They will like you. I just know they will.

I will have to have another tooth pulled as it is starting to decay. If I keep on, I will be all out of teeth. Haha. Would you like a toothless husband? I don't think that will happen so don't worry. Well, it is about eating time so I will finish this afterward. I sure wish I was eating with you. It would feel more like eating.

Well, I am back and will try to finish now. We had chuck roast, potatoes and gravy for dinner. We also had coffee and bread and butter with a salad and canned peaches. You don't know how much I wish we could be together.

We are going to have formation in a minute, so I got to close and get my gun., cartridge belt, gas mask and steel helmet on. Boy, when we get all our equipment on, we look like a walking battle wagon. Wish you could see us in full war dress sometime. We weigh about ninety pounds more. You would get a kick out of it. We just had a trial run just for practice in case we have an attack.

We ran about eighty rods and walked a mile. We will probably never see an attack.

How is every one getting along there? Every thing here is going along but I wish I could be there with you and be of more use and help to you and I in our life to come. I would like to get our house started together as soon as I can so we could work for ourselves and have plenty in our later lives. If we work it right, we can assure ourselves of having plenty in our later life when we can't work anymore. I would have enough, ourselves. I want our lives to be a happy one until the end of our lives and if we pull together we can have it that way.

My sister was right. If you make me happy as you have done, there isn't anything I wouldn't do to make you happy. That is the way I want you to be if I can. I know you will do all you can to make me happy. That is all I can ask of you.

Honey, I must close, as I must wash out some clothes. My sis said I was always Mom's favorite boy. The reason for that was I always treated her good. I helped her all I could and tried to make her life as nice as I could. I have spent enough money, when I worked, on her. If I would have it now I would have enough to set up a home for us and a lot besides. That is why she liked me so well.

But I always said that when I got married, I would not be dependent on anyone. We will make our own way when we get together again for good. I know my parents would help us in any way they could but we can make our own way as soon as I am out of here.

Your folks are doing good having you with them while I am in the army. Someday, we can give it back to them. We can try awful hard to anyway. I will do all I can for us. As long as I am with the army, it will be slow coming through. But we will get it sooner or later. I can't rush the government but sure would like to. I know you know that I am not lying or trying to kid you if it takes longer than I hope. As you said in your letter, I now have someone who will always believe in me and I will always love you dearly if I can find you waiting for me.

So until we meet again, I will always love you.

Your Loving Husband, C.W. Ward SWAK

P.S. I have not written that woman yet, but I will.

My Wife, Cora Mae, I Love You,

Dearest Wife,

I got your two letters of the 4th & 5th. I am sorry about that money order. I sent to town with one of the boys to get it and then I was going to send it on to you. But when he came back, he had telegraphed it to you. I knew right then it was going to cause you some problems and bother to get it. I won't let that happen again.

Dear, about that baptism . . . I was baptized a long time ago in a Methodist church. I guess once is enough. What church were you baptized in?

Honey about that money for a furlough. I haven't saved any money for a furlough. If I get a furlough you will have to send me some. Don't worry about it. It ain't none of my business but how much are you saving? I can't see how you can save on no more than I am sending you. I sure will be glad when you get that allotment. You will get more money and what you do with that money is okay by me as long as you do what's right. If I do get a furlough and you can't send money, I will get it some other way.

Let me know what church you were baptized in? How is our family coming along? One time baptizing is enough and alright with me. I pray every night and try to be a good boy every day. I'd sure hate to die before you and I get to live our life. But God will decide that for us. He knows best. We must have belief in Him.

Don't worry about letters from my folks. They are slow to write. You didn't write anything to hurt them. I know they are glad I married you, now. They were afraid I would wind up with someone that was no good. They know you will make a good wife for me. Just as I know it.

I've got to go to work. I am working nights. I will write tomorrow. For now, I will say I love you. Honey, I just heard our president speak over the radio. He said we were going to win this war as soon as possible. Who knows? I just hope it ends this year. Every one seems to think it will.

Honey, always remember that I love you. So long, for now. Tell everyone I wish I were there to give them a big hug. When I do get back, I am going to get a kiss for everyday I am away from you. So you can look forward to that. Can you stand that many kisses at one time. Haha. I hope you can. There will be many more than that when I get through. But, I will never get through.

Well, another day and everything is as usual. I hope all is okay there. We had to bake two hundred dozen rolls and thirty sheet cakes last night. We also cut twenty three hundred pork chops up. We were pretty busy.

Honey, I don't think you are nagging me one bit wanting me to get baptized. I know everyone should be and I am glad I was. I know you are trying to get your husband to be a good boy and I am trying to be a good boy. So whenever you want to tell me anything, go right ahead and tell me. I won't think you are nagging at me. I need someone to keep me straightened out.

I think my brother will get all my rights on the farm. Like you say he isn't married or anything and with his helpless arm, it is better that he does.

I am glad your mother likes me. I will always try to make your people like me and most of all, you. Honey we need to get the birth certificate straightened out for Louise. It may be of use for her someday.

I'm glad you say you would walk to the mailbox with me again. I would anytime as long as it was you who went with me. That is the truth and I will never regret going there with you on the first day we met.

Do you remember when we went to catch the bus to Nashville, that day? We walked out by the bridge while we waited for the bus. We sat by the side of the road by the trees. We talked of marriage and I told you I would like to but I didn't have enough money. The real reason was that I was afraid. You looked so pretty and were so sweet to me, there by the road under the trees. I couldn't help falling in love with you. And I will remember that all my life. We only saw each other once before we were married. When we first met, it seemed as if I always knew you. Remember, on the bus when I started to make love to you just like we had gone together a long time. You made me stop teasing Jr. Honey, that is a God sent memory for me. All in all, I want to thank God for giving you to me. I mean that with all my heart.

For now, I must close and go over to eat, as it is dinnertime. Honey, if I write something you don't understand, write and ask me about it. And don't be afraid of thinking you are nagging me. I only wish I was there so you could nag me in person. Always remember I love you more than anything else in the world.

I Love You, Your husband Charles

June, 1942

To My Darling Wife, Cora Mae,

I am on guard now and I have two hours to wait until I have to walk my post. So while I wait, I will try to write a few lines to you in between my shift and let you know how to goes with me.

I will try to get back to the kitchen if I can. I don't know if I can get my rating back or not. I will have to be an awful good boy for a while though. I will try to get an allotment made out for you if I can. It can't do any harm to try it. I am using a flashlight to see to write this letter. It won't hurt to try to get it and get a break. It will make a difference to you and our lives together when this conflict is over.

Tell your folks I promise to do everything I can to make your life as full and happy as possible. I want to prove to people that I did not marry you just to satisfy my desires and passion. I really believe I have found love and companionship with you. And that with one, without the other, neither could live a truly happy life. As you know, Honey, every human being has a mate to go through life with and I truly believe you and I was put on this earth for that purpose. Honey, there is nothing more holy than true love and companionship. I sincerely believe that no matter what the circumstances it has to be obtained, people should work and fight for it. That is one big reason we are at war. So don't ever give up because you and I will get our goal if we fight together. Honey, if we keep our life on the straight and narrow, we will always find happiness together, no matter what happens or how hard it gets for us. Please answer in your next letter if you think I am right or wrong.

I can't think of much more to say right now except if only I could tell you in writing how much happiness you have brought to me and for the one chance to prove I believe in you. To prove beyond doubt my love for you to all the people who ever has a reason to have doubts of me. So, Darling, don't ever let anything come between us until I have had my rightful chance to prove myself to you. Will you promise to do that?

I guess I will close for now, as I will never be able to explain my feelings for you in writing of my full love for you. I will have to prove myself some other way. So until I write again, I say from one who only wants to be your true love and companion for the rest of his life.

From your devoted and very lonesome husband,

Charles Wesley Ward

Tell everyone I said hello and give the children my love. I only live for you now. I love you SWAK

1942

To The Best Wife I Ever Had, Cora Mae,

Well I just finished writing to you, but I keep thinking of you so much it will give my mind ease to write again. I don't know what to write about, so I will make it up as I go along.

Your mother was right when she said it would be harder for us if we got married when we did. I haven't missed a night yet when I go to bed thinking and wondering of you and what you are doing, how you are feeling and all kind of things.

I am sitting in my bed, writing to you. Everyone else has gone over to the canteen or to town. I don't go if I feel out of place because you are not with me. Life has a different meaning since we got married. To be out here is about ten times harder without you since we got married. You won't never realize what you have made me see. It makes a difference to a person when they know there is someone out there in the world that wants to be with them. Honey, I knew for a long time that I wanted you, but like I said, I was afraid of being married. I was afraid I would not be man enough to keep up my side of the bargain. Or be good to my wife. I was afraid I would be a poor husband and not be able to love my wife like I should.

But now, I know no matter what happens or where we are at, whether we are together or apart, there will never be any doubt in my mind of my love for you. I know I would not mistreat you or do anything to make you feel bad toward me. If I ever do, I want you to come out and tell me because if I cause hurt to you, it will be because I did not know what I was doing. I will never knowingly do anything that would stop you from loving me. You are the only one that can make me stop loving you. I don't think you will or could do that.

I will always be proud of you, if you will let me and not do anything that will make me feel bad of you. You were really disappointed in me when I was with you. I didn't mean for you to take it that way. I want people to know I love you and am proud of you. But I wasn't use to having a wife to take with me or to show people I loved her. I will always stand up for you and show your folks I am proud to have you as my wife. I will prove that to people no matter where I am. You will always be the Cora Mae I met on the bus.

I can't possible tell you how much I love you, so I will close. Someday, you will see that we were meant for each other. Never, will I regret a day of our marriage.

So until I write again, I love you, Charles SWAK

My folks always call me Wes, but I like Charles better. That is why Skeet called me Wes in her letter. I always call my sis, Skeet. Answer soon.

1942

Well, being as I have time on my hand, I will write. I wrote last night and you will have gotten that letter before you get this. So, maybe you will have some idea of how I feel about you. As you can probably tell from reading my letter that I can't explain myself very well in writing. I hope it is good enough, until I can get a chance to prove myself to you, otherwise.

As tomorrow is Sunday, I will make this letter short and write to you tomorrow. Honey, write as often as you can, won't you? Tell the children I said hello and give each of them a kiss, Betty, Louise and Jr. And lots of good wishes to them, too.

Well, I can't think of much more to say right now. I am sending some picture post cards of places we passed through on our way back home. I hope you will like them. I think you will.

Well, I will close for now and so until I write again, I love you and always will.

Yours Forever,

Your husband, C.W.Ward

SWAK Be good for me, Honey. Tell your folks I said hello. What is Jesse doing these days? Tell him to watch that girl of his, haha. How is Robert doing with his traps? How are Bill and his girl coming along? Getting ready for matrimony, too?

1942

To The Swellest Girl I Ever Knew. Cora Mae,

Here I am again. Nothing to do, as it is a Sunday and we have that day off and plenty of time to write,

I asked my folks to send my gun to you if they don't need it. They probably will send it to you, though. If your brothers use it, ask them to take care of it for me. I am still waiting for a letter from you. How is everyone there? I am okay except for my lonesomeness for you. How are you feeling now? Okay, I hope. I will be glad when this war is over, don't you?

I guess I might go back to cooking. They say "once a cook always a cook". I just don't seem satisfied out with the troops anyway. Time goes faster in the kitchen.

The sun sure is shining bright here today. Wonder how it is there? Boy, I can remember and never will forget us standing by that car in Franklin. I felt as though I was dying, having to leave you. I was afraid if I didn't have you get in the car so I could hold you, I would have died right there. That was the hardest thing I had to do and I hope I don't have to go through that again. The mail call just came in and I am holding my breath hoping to get a letter from you.

I just got your letter, Honey. Boy, am I glad to hear from you. If you are happy, then I know I made you love me. You have made me the happiest boy there ever was and I know we are fitted for one another if you are happy to have me as your husband. I know I am proud to have you as my wife. The only thing that was wrong was having to leave you.

Tell Odell he couldn't have felt worse than I did having to go. Tell him hello and good luck. He sure was nice to me and I was proud of it. Tell your folks I said hello and good luck to them, too. Tell Jr. I am glad he liked the pretty we bought for him. Give them all a big squeeze for me.

Well, Honey, I'll close as I am about out of anything to say. So long and hope to see you soon.

Yours Forever,

Your husband, C.W. Ward I Love You SWAK

1942

My Darling Wife & Bride,

I got your letter and was glad to get it as I am with all your letters.

First, let me explain to you about what I meant about our marriage certificate. I wanted to tell you how to get a copy of it by a notary public who will copy it on another paper so it will be legal. A photographic copy is made by a studio or camera. I am glad you sent the marriage license instead so you don't have to worry about it. I can do it here so it won't cause you any trouble. Then, I can put in for your allotment that I want you to have.

I am glad you are not in the family way as that would be unfair to you. I would probably be away from you at the worst time. I would want to be there as that is where I should be. You and I should be together when something like that is going on. So I am glad you are okay. I am praying everyday that I can get close to you and no one can take you away from me. I am trusting in you to do right by me and be true.

You know, Honey, your ex would only cause you trouble in the end if you did go back to him, so I am believing in you to not even think about going back to him.

I have to finish this tomorrow. Well, I can finish it now. Honey, don't worry about my folks. If they are mad at us, then we will wait until they get over it. I got no fear of them getting mad. They will write you. They are just a little slow at writing. Anyway you are my wife and I love you and if they don't, it won't matter much. My sis will write to you soon enough. I just sent her your address last week.

Darling, this is my first letter to you in three days. I guess I am getting lazy again. I hope when I get back to you, you don't hold it against me for the way when I was with you. I had been away from you for so long and I had not been with another woman. I just was so glad to see you that I couldn't help myself. But it will be different when we are together all the time. But, I will always remember how good you treated me while I was there.

I can't think of much to say right now. No matter what happens or where you are, you will always be the girl I love. You make my life happy. I truly love you.

Your Husband, Charles XOXO

(Author's note. A "pretty' is a southern word for toy.)

1942

I am laying down writing this, which is why it is so sloppy. Please excuse it even though at times you might have to guess at what I am trying to say.

Honey, I know you are worried about my folks and whether they will like you or not. I will take you to see them sometime and when they see you then they will know the reason I love you. I can't help it. It is all your fault. If you hadn't been so nice and sweet to me and treated me so kind, I would not have been your husband.

So, you see, it is your fault. And Darling, I am so glad you were that way. You have made me the happiest fellow in the world. You also made me see a new way of life of happiness for me. I never was happy before we were married. You have done a world of good for me and I don't know how to repay you. But I will try for the rest of my life, God willing.

Honey, don't worry what I think when you show your love for me. Honey, if you show your love for someone, that is all the more reason for them to keep trying to make you happy. So they will keep on loving you and that is what I want you to do. It makes me happy that you want people to know how much we love each other and it doesn't matter how much you carry on or where you do it. It shows you love me.

That is all that counts, that we love one another. You got your own way of life and I love it. Your ways are the reason I love you because they are nice ways to have. Honey, any man would be proud of you. You are the only girl who could mean so much to me, so believe me when I say I really worship you. You are all I live for, so be good and I will love you, no matter what happens.

Well, Honey, I am off duty for now and have run out of things to say. When you receive the letter with the money, let me know. It could get lost, so until I hear from you so I know it is okay. Let me know if it is all there, too. There was a fifty-dollar bill, two twenty-dollar bills and a ten-dollar bill.

Tell the children I said hello and send them all my love. Tell your folks I said hello.

Well, I must close for now, so answer soon. WAK

Good Luck, Your Husband

(Author's note. Mom's insecurities stemmed from the fact that she was a divorced mother of three at a time and area where this was almost considered scandalous. Dad's insecurities stemmed from the fact that Mom remained in close proximity with her ex.)

(Fragment)

I would like to be near you. I get sick in my heart from missing and wanting to be with you. Someday, I am going to be one happy boy. It can't come too soon to suit me. I've got you to look forward to. I love you so much. Knowing you are waiting for me gives me the faith to go on so I can come back to you. Then I can have more of the happiest life I ever knew. Darling, always remember that I love you. And Honey, always be true to me and I will do the same for you.

So Bye, I love you, C.W.Ward SWAK

To The One I Am Longing For Today, Cora Mae, I Love You,

Well, it is Sunday now and I will write a little more and send it with the one I just wrote. I guess I will go to church tonight as we have a minister coming in. Wish you were here to go with me. It is a bright sunny day today and I wish you were here for me to hold in my arms. I can just feel you in my heart. I sure get lonesome for you. You can't imagine the delight it would be to have you here.

Your Loving Husband,

Charles SWAK

P.S. I guess you know that we are at war now.

1942,

Well, I am late getting started writing tonight so I will have to make this short. But, sweet I hope. I got your letter today telling me that Bill got married. I hope he is in love with his wife as I am with mine. I also hope he ain't as confused and backward as I was that first night as I was with you and hope his wife is as sweet and nice to him as you were to me. He won't never forget it if she is. Give him all my best wishes and good luck and all the happiness in the world.

Honey, I sure wish I could be with you tonight. I would squeeze you to death or nearly so. I can just feel you in my arms now. I never will forget our first week together, so Honey, keep your chin up and be good.

Bye for now.

Your Husband Charles

I love you, SWAK

(fragmented letter)

Would you like to flip a nickel to decide on whether we would be better off in Ohio. Whatever you say will be alright by me. One place or another makes me no difference. We will be happy anyplace where you are. If you don't want to do the deciding, it is okay by me. But Honey, whoever does decide between us, each one of us I mean, must promise forever not to hold it against the other.

So, Honey, I will finish this tonight and mail it tomorrow.

Well, I will finish this now. We got paid yesterday and I will send you some money. I hope this gets to you better than the last time. I will go get the money order myself. Maybe I will do a better job of it.

Honey, I sure wish I could be there with you. Today and for the rest of my life. I sure do a lot of thinking about you. We sure will be happy when we do get to live together. I received the cookies and liked them very much.

(End of fragment)

To The Only. One I Will Ever Want, My Darling Wife, Cora Mae,

Well, Honey, I just finished a letter to your sis, so I will proceed to write you a few lines. Everything here is about as usual. I got your present today and was proud to get it. The mirror was bent a little bit around the frame but not broke. I really did appreciate getting it.

Honey, we are going to move somewhere and in the near future. I don't know when but until I write you just send your letters here. Boy, I sure am lonesome tonight. Wish I could be with you. My spirits would be higher.

I wrote a letter to your mother. I hope she gets it. Honey, tell them to write to me often and I will try to answer them. Tell your brothers to write, too. I get awful lonesome when I don't get letters from people back there. My folks don't write very often, so by all of you writing, it makes it a lot better.

You know, when I get out of here I won't even volunteer for the Salvation Army. Ain't I awful? Haha

I want you to be sure and let me know if you got that sixty-dollar money order I sent you. I also hope you liked those little step-ins. Haha. I also wish I could be there to take someone's, I know, down. Could I or couldn't I?

Honey, do you think you are going to like having a hair brain like me around for the rest of your life? But someone has to put up with me and I hope you will take that job. I promise not to be any worse than I ever was. Do you promise to take the job?

Honey, tell everyone I said hello and give our children my love. Say! I hope the busy bodies keep minding their business. They will if they know what is good for them. Does your ex ever come out anymore to see you?

My sis must have had her baby as I ain't heard from her in two weeks. I'll bet it is a girl. What do you say? What do you think our first one will be? I hope they will be twins or triplets. What do you hope? I'll bet that would be fun for both of us. I know it would be for me. Ain't I awful?

But anyway, I am glad I have a wife I can talk like that with. I am glad I wouldn't get kicked out of bed as I don't like to be kicked around, anyway. I wouldn't want a hound to get kicked around. Would you kick him? Don't mind me. I get that way once in awhile. You know my dad said one time that if my head were full of dynamite, there wouldn't be enough to blow my nose. Do you think he was right?

The weather sure has been nice out here the last couple of days. I sure hope to get a furlough soon as I am getting very anxious to be with you. I can hardly wait.

So, my Darling Sweetheart, I'll close for now, saying I love you more than anything else in this world. With all my heart and soul, so long, and good night. I'll write tomorrow evening.

I Love You,

Your Husband, Charles

I cut a clipping from the paper. Wish I could rub my wife a little. Would the sparks fly then? Haha. I wonder.

God Bless You Charles

1942

To The Sweetest Girl I Know, My Wife, Cora Mae,

Honey, you probably wondered why I broke off so suddenly in my last letter. Well, one of the boys said he was going into town to get some supplies, so I went with him. You will probably get that letter earlier as I mailed it from there. Now I will continue with this one.

Honey, if you are having any trouble, let me know. How are the children getting along? Boy, I wish I could be there with you and them. That would make me so happy. We would probably be arguing all the time about who will get out of bed first, especially on a cold winter morning. Do you think so?

How is Bill getting along in his married life? I sure hope Robert is not taken into the army. He shouldn't be taken off the farm as short as farmers are these days and is needed there.

Does your old boyfriend come around anymore? I'll bet he is just like anyone else. He just can't help from wanting to see you. I'll bet he wishes he could have gotten to marry you instead of me. I can see why. All men would like to have a nice wife, so he would like to have you. Remember how you said the boys would look at you in town and whistle. Maybe he is thinking of those pink lips, too. Haha.

Bet anyone would whistle at you if they knew you like I do. Don't you? Boy, I wish I could be there to whistle at you. I would whistle at more than those pink lips. I would whistle just to hold you in my arms and kiss you. Honey, don't get mad at the way I talk. You know how men are. But I really am proud of my wife. I didn't marry you just so I could sleep with you for a week. I married you because I loved you like I never loved anybody in my life.

Do you remember the night we slept down at your brother's house? I'll never forget that night. I really did enjoy that night even though I was in the wrong state of mind. And didn't get what I wanted. Do you remember it? I am sorry now that I had you figured wrong that night I met you. Please don't think bad of me. I am very glad now that I was wrong, aren't you? It would have been bad for both of us if I had been right. You just don't know how glad I was that you were the way you were when I met you. I would not have had the wife I have if you had been the other way. So see what you have done to me and yourself by being a good girl. You got yourself a lot of trouble to contend with the rest of your life. Haha.

Darling, you know the way I love you. If we are anyway near fair with each other we will always love one another as we do now. I know you are the only one that God created for me. So do you think my mother-in-law's daughter will give me a kiss in her next letter. Please? I got the page of kisses you sent me. I wish I could give you a real kiss right now. I would probably be so happy I would bite your lips too hard. You will never know just how much I love you.

So now I will close saying I love you. Tell everyone I said hello and give the children a hug for me.

Darling, I just got your letter today and was glad to get it and will answer in this one. I am glad you got my folks' present and hope you will like it. Now, I want you to go ahead and use it if you need it. But think of me all the time you use it. I want you to get the good of it.

I hate to admit this, but just as I told you, the chances of me coming out of this war alive is slim. The true facts often hurts us.

But the war is the only one with human lives. But we don't want to think of that. It will only be harder for both of us. Now, I don't want you to worry of me and if I am lost in this war, we will meet again in heaven. So, Darling, we can hope and pray to God then if we come out together, we will know that he made us for each other. So keep praying and I will do the same. But if I lose, know that I will die happy. You have made me that way. There is nothing I can do that will repay you for what you have done for me. I know if I do get to come back to you, I will be a happy man

We are getting ready to move out now. By the time you get this, we will be in Santa Rosa. I signed my payroll today so that means it will be another month before I can do anything about the allotment. I'll send you some money later on in the month.

Well, Darling, I guess I had better close now as it is getting late. So answer soon and remember that I love you.

Your husband, Charles SWAK XOXOX DARLING I LOVE YOU.

1942

To My Darling Wife, Cora Mae Ward, I Love You.

Well, just a line to say hello and that everything is going okay here for me. I am going to help cook roast turkey tonight as tomorrow is Thanksgiving Day. If you have turkey, think of me.

Got a letter from home and they asked me a few questions and wished us all the happiness in the world. They asked the children's ages and if your people were farm folks. I guess they are not mad or anything. My people don't have much use for girls who live in cities. They like farm people best. You should be getting a letter from my brother. I would like very much to know what he says if you will tell me.

How are you these days? Don't forget to let me know about yourself. How are your folks? I am kind of lonesome tonight. We are going to move out of this camp again. Can't say where as that is part of regulations. But as soon as I can, I will let you know. I don't worry over it because it won't be going across, I don't think. Just to a new camp.

Honey you don't know how I love you. I sure look to the day when I can come back to you. That will be a happy day for me. Don't forget to have a copy made of that marriage license. Or else send me the license and I will have it done. I would also like to have a picture of you and I will send you one of me. I will send you and your mother those engraved pillow cases as soon as I can. I've got to wait until I get paid first, though, as my money is low from my furlough. But I had a swell time on it, anyway. I also got the one thing I wanted most in my life . . . . YOU!

Well, Honey, I've got to close. Write often as I crave your letters. Tell the children hello for me.

Your Husband, Charles SWAK

Dearest Wife,

Well, Honey, I am on guard now. It is seven o'clock Sunday night. I will write a short letter now and send it with the one I wrote last night. You probably will think I am silly but it seems like it has been ten years since I was with you. The time sure goes slow. We will be a happy pair when this war is over and we are together again.

I was walking my post about three o'clock this morning and I saw a soldier in a car along the road making love to a girl. It sure made me wish you were here, loving me, too. Someday, we will be together again and we can do our own loving the rest of our lives. We will know what being apart means so we will take care not to let things pull us apart. Honey, I hope when you get this that you are not as lonesome as I am while writing it.

Honey, did my mother ever write you?

I can't think of much else to write, so I will close. I will write more tomorrow. Tell your brother I said I think of him everyday and wish I could be there with him. But I can't until I get out of here and that won't happen until we make peace in this world again. I think that Germany is about whipped now, but Japan is still going strong. Italy isn't much of an obstacle. Maybe with a little luck, we will soon be on our way with our lives.

Dad told me that he would rather fight two wars than be married. That was before I came into the army. Do you think he was right? Am I going to have to fight with you? I bet not. Haha. You would see how much I would fight you. I would just spank you and let you go. I bet you think I couldn't give you a spanking. But, who knows? You don't need to think I would ever mistreat you, though. I was just joking.

Honey, I will close for now. There is no news and I can't think of much more to say. Tell your sister I said hello. Kiss the children for me. How are they feeling? Hope they are alright. I really think of you and them lot. I sure hope I can be a good father to them as that would make it a lot better for us and that is the way we want it to be.

So Darling, as always, I love you,

Your husband, Charles SWAK XOXO

1942

To My Sweetheart, Forever & Ever, My Wife, Cora Mae, I Love You,

Well, another day has come and gone and the war ain't over yet. Honey, the time sure drags by. You asked how I liked the cake? Well, I haven't got no cake yet. You said in a letter before you were sending me a package. It must have got lost. Maybe we will have better luck next time.

It sure will be okay with me if you write foolish things in your letters. I like to read your foolish things. You write any foolish thing you care to write. It suits me. I would like to be there to read the funny papers in bed with you. Would you like me to? Haha. Bill can take Polly's pants down all he wants. I just want to be able to do likewise with someone I know. Do you know who I mean? Bill and Polly can't enjoy themselves anymore than I did our first married week together. Did you enjoy yourself, too?

Tell them to have lots of fun while they are young. Tell them good luck from me. You and I will have our day and when it comes we will have lots of reasons for us to be very happy, won't we? Darling, you can't imagine how much you mean to me. I am only glad you love me, which makes me very happy. I sure wish I was there so we could share that shirt of yours. I would be very happy and more to pull off your panties. I would try more if you would let me. I really would. Haha.

I just got a haircut. I feel a little bald. Did you ever hear of the fellow who went to the doctor to get examine? When he came back, his wife asked him about it. He told her the doctor said that he was fit as a fiddle. And that he was one hundred fifty pounds of living dynamite. She said, "Yes, but you only got a three-inch fuse". Haha. Don't mind my corny jokes.

Well, Darling, I can't think of much else to say as everything is as usual. I helped bake two hundred dozen rolls last night. That is a lot of rolls. They feed twenty three hundred men in the kitchen where I am going to cook school. This is an embark station camp.

Well, Sweetheart, tell everyone I said hello and give the children my love. Always remember I love you. Honest I do.

From one who is always longing for you,

Your husband, Charles SWAK I Love You.

To The One I Love, Cora Mae,

Well I received your letter and was glad to get it. Honey, if you want to get a calf or pig, I think it is a good idea. And if you want to move, go ahead. Just do as you think best and I know we both will agree on it. You know it may be a long time before I can come home and live with you. But I think you will be okay with Bill and Polly. I am going to raise heck if they don't get that allotment through pretty quick so you can be self supporting.

Honey, I don't want you to think I am not satisfied with your sex. I knew there would be no maiden head or cherry, as some call it. My love for you is far too strong for that to hold me back. We had a short arm inspection the other day. I passed as I had not been anywhere to get any diseases of that sort. You know what I mean by "short arm" don't you? Haha.

Honey, if you move, let me know how you are getting along from day to day as I worry about you. I really do. I love you so much that I don't know what I would do if anything happened or went wrong for you. You needn't thank me for the money. Just tell me that you love me and that is payment enough and more than anything else could. Tell your brothers I am glad for them and wish I could be there, too.

You won't ever quit loving me, will you? Promise me that. Honey, honest, I mean everything I say when I say I love you and very thing else I say. I am just as proud and happy you are my wife as anyone can be. It doesn't matter how hard and dark things seem, I will always be happy if you are my wife. Having a nice wife is everything to a man and Darling, you are a nice wife.

About the words on the back of your picture, yes Honey, I would marry you all over again anytime and I would like to sleep with you. Does that answer it? God knows I love you. I sure wish I could be there with you more than anything else in the world. I hope when you get this, the weather will have changed and your cold is over with. We sure will be happy when we can live together. That will be one happy day for us.

I must close for now, so tell everyone I said hello. Tell the children hello, too.

Good-bye, I love you. If I ain't answered all your questions well enough, let me know.

I Love You Honest I do.

Your Husband, Charles SWAK

Green Springs, Ohio

Dear Wes,

So you went and got married while I was wringing my hands in fear of you being sent overseas. Aren't you sorry you didn't let me know about it? All joking aside, I hope you both will be very happy.

And you will if you don't let outsiders interfere. Mom was like an exploded bomb I guess. She said little but not much. Dad said he was just glad you married this one instead of the last girl you had. They will either get over it and if not they can get under it. It must have been rather sudden, wasn't it? Or did you have it all doped out? Write me about it and if you think I am too damn inquisitive, let me know. I love you like the brother you are and want to be a friend to you both.

Well, Dad was here to Granny's over the weekend. He brought her some black walnuts for her cookies. He got a ham in return. I'm glad he, Alice, Grandpa, Morris, Helen and Tyler had dinner here Sunday. Alice stayed here all night Sunday. Carl took her to the show that evening. I stayed home and cleaned up the house and gave Nelson and myself a bath and then went to bed. I was so tired.

Jean and Harry came in around five o'clock, just as we were starting to eat. Carl and Harry got a pheasant and two rabbits the first day of hunting. We dressed and cooked all three of them for Sunday dinner and supper.

Queenie caught one pheasant and Carl is so puffed up over it. You couldn't buy her for a hundred dollars now. He was offered twenty-five dollars but he wouldn't sell her. I could have wrung his neck but what could I have done about it?

I washed yesterday and had them on the line before daylight. First time in my life. Then it rained just as the sun came up. I had to bring them in and dry them all in the house. Boy, what a mess!

We went hunting all day Thanksgiving Day. Carl and Potter hunted in the morning and Helen, Nelson and I planned on going out in the afternoon unless they got so many birds and rabbits that we would have to had to stay home to clean them. No danger of that happening though.

Dad said Earl bought himself a thirty-six or seven coupe. Dad said he left Thursday and four gallons of gas would probably take him a long way.

Well, I must close and write to Jean. Write me even though you are an old married man now. Even if it is only a note.

Lots of happiness and no trouble to the both of you. We mean that honestly and sincerely.

From,

Carl, Louise& Nelson

1942

My Dearest Wife,

I got a letter from my folks today. They didn't have much to say except for a few questions. They want to keep my gun until the end of November season up there and then they will send it to you if that would be alright for you. That way my brother could use it for another season of hunting.

Honey in that letter I wrote you . . . if I said anything wrong you can tell me of it. I just got angry when I read about him and maybe I said too much. I'm sorry if I did. If he causes you any trouble, you do what you think best.

I've got to stand guard duty tonight so I will write more later. Tell all your people I said hello. Also, the children. I get my picture taken Monday. I hope they are good so I can send them to you. I want one of you, so if you can, send one to me.

Honey, I sure could stand to be with you tonight for I am lonesome for your love. I can't explain it but if I don't stop thinking in my mind about you all the time, I fear I will go out of my head. Now I know what your mother was saying when she said it would be better to wait to marry after the war was over, as that would make it harder. But I will never regret it, will you? Maybe we ain't apart for too long now, anyway. I hope not. You don't know what it would mean to me to be back with you for good.

I am on guard now so I must close. Will write more later.

I love you truly,

C.W.Ward SWAK

To the One I Love,

I sent you some money. Did you receive it? Honey, you said in your letter that Robert had to go and take a blood test for the army. Boy, if they take both your brothers, it will be hard on your folks. Your father ought to go to the draft board and try to get them an exemption, as he needs them on the farm. The draft board will let him have a six-month deferment. I think they should, anyway. It won't hurt and they couldn't lose anything to try.

I sure hate of any one to have to go into the army. It is hard for anyone to get use to it, although I am getting use to it by now. The first hard part is homesickness, which takes about six month to get over. Then comes learning military law, courtesy and discipline. There isn't anything hard about it, just hard to get use to. Don't tell them I said this but the best way to get on is to do only what you are told to do and don't do what you are not told to. Always obey orders from anyone higher up in rank and the rest will come by instinct.

I've been in the army two years come March 13th and I am still a rookie. Tell your brothers not to worry about the shots as they don't hurt as bad as some say. It's like taking a blood test. I have had at least fifteen shots since I have been in the army and about six of them when I was in the C.C.C. None of them hurt very much.

Well, when you get this, I hope you will also have gotten my previous letters. And know from them that no matter what goes on or what others say, what your past life was or anything else, I am loving and believing in you until you see different yourself. I married you because I loved you and believed in you. What your past life was or mine was makes no difference. It never will. I know you don't love your ex-husband and I am very proud to have you as my wife. I swear to God, Honey, I love you more than anything in the world. Our future is all that matters to us. And I want that to be just the way you, the children and I want it to be as we are the only ones that count now. Other people are out.

So, Darling, don't ever think I don't love you because I do and I don't care what other people say about it. The only thing I ask is that you be the same Cora Mae that I married and we will always love one another as long as we have anything to say about it. And we do. This is the way I believe. If we ever do wrong to each other it will come out without other people's interference. So, don't let your ex or anything concerning him worry you, as far as my love for you. He is a thing of that past and the past does not concern me. So you can believe this, I love you and nothing else matters to me.

Well, I have to close for now and when you get this, I hope you can say to yourself and really believe that 'Charles truly does love me". Please don't be doubtful of that.

Your husband now and always, Charles I Love You

1942

To The One I Love,

I received your letter tonight and was glad to get it. Honey, if you use all the money, it is okay by me. Please use it any way you want. That is why I sent it to you. If you need to use what you have in the bank, go ahead. Fix up your home anyway you want. If it takes all the money, that is okay by me. Darling, I don't care how you use it. Just so it is what you want and you are happy. All I care about in this world is to make you happy. The money and how you spend it is the least worry. I only wish I could send more

I am glad you asked about the allotment. I ain't heard anything about it. If I don't hear soon, I am going to raise hell with someone, pardon the expression. It should not be too long, now. I know you think I am sending you too much money that I need, but that is my worry, not yours.

So Honey, you get your house fixed up anyway you want. When I get the allotment through, I will be able to save for my furlough. The only thing that worries me is the time between when they take my money out and add to it. Because then I won't get much and won't be able to send you but very little. I won't be able to send enough to keep you going until you start to get the allotment. If that happens and you get low on money, let me know and I will see you get enough to get along on. But I am trying to get it so that won't happen. I hope I can anyway.

Honey, I've got to close for now, as it is time for lights out. I will try to write more tomorrow and say a few things more. Honey, all I care about is that you are happy and have room in your heart for me. Please don't worry of me. I will be alright.

So, I will close saying I love you dearly and truly.

Love, Charles

P.S. When can I get a big red kiss?

1943

To The One Who is as Sweet as Honey to Me.

Dearest Cora Mae,

Well I guess I will write to see if you are okay. I haven't heard from you in four days. I hope you haven't forgotten where I live. I am writing this at two o'clock in the morning. I just got off duty and thought I would write. I am looking for a letter from you every day. I sure hope I get one tomorrow. I got one from my uncle that was mailed on the fifth of January. It sure had been everywhere but where it should have been.

Honey, I saw a boy from my camp today. He says they haven't started giving out furloughs yet. It doesn't look as if we will get one soon. But don't think I ain't anxious for one. How is everything going by you, anyhow? Okay? I sure hope so, anyway. I wouldn't want my wife to be otherwise.

Well, Honey, I've got to make this short. Things just go on in the same old way, anyhow. Just the same old routine, day in and day out. I just had to go over to the barracks to get a stamp to send this out. I am writing this in the kitchen office. When I came back another kid was reading this letter. The lights are all out in our barracks.

I hope your brothers are okay in getting their work done. I only wish I could be there with them. How are the children getting along? Tell them I said hello to them.

Well, Honey, I will close for now. Hoping to hear from you soon. I am a little sleepy tonight to talk of much foolishment tonight. So, always I am loving you more than anything in the world.

Your husband, Charles

My address will remain the same for another month as far as I know. So keep sending your letters here to me. Answer soon. SWAK

1943

To My Loved One, Cora Mae,

I love you. Well, honey, I will write in answer to your three letters that I received today. I sure was glad to get them. You know, I thought it was longer than four months since we were together. It seems more like four years since I last saw you.

Honey, you do not need worry about anyone or anything anyone said about your past. All I want is you, just as you are. As long as you are honest with me then the past is out and doesn't matter. I will always love you just like I do now. So let's forget out past lives. What people say won't bother either of us now. You don't need to worry about letting you down, cause I love you too much for that. I will always be the same fellow that you married and I will always treat the children just like any father could. I will always love you just as I do now. If anything, I will love you more. All I ask is that you play the game square and be honest with me. Then I can be sure we will be happy. I promise you, I will always love you and the children.

Honey, I imagine it is hard for you to get use to the way I am with you and the children. Your having the children never will make any difference to me. Please don't think of that. You love them and

I love them too. I want you to understand that I am happy with my marriage and intend to make it happy for the children and you as I possibly can. You see, I have four loves, counting the children and you and I want to have a happy life with you. So don't worry about my not loving you. I hope you can understand what I mean. Love is stronger than anything in this world and my love for you is as true as it can be.

Tell Bill not to work too hard. He may be like the honeybee was. It went out and worked hard all that day and when he came home that night, he was too tired to make his honey. Do you get it? The lady barber told me that when she was cutting my hair one time.

Well, Honey, I must close as it is time to go on duty. We made three thousand six hundred sandwiches last night and thirty-two peach pies. Boy, we sure had to work fast. We started about eight o'clock last night and got done at six o'clock this morning.

Tell all I said good luck and hello. Give the children my love and best wishes. Honey, I will always love you, no matter what comes along and I mean that. So get that idea that I may be tired of you off your mind, please.

So for now I will say so long.

From your husband, Charles SWAK XOXO

1942

To The One I Love, My Wife, Cora Mae,

As the day has waned and wandered and is almost over, I guess I will try and write a few lines. We had three fairly large meals to get out and it really kept us busy. Boy, I sure wish I was back in civilian life. I sure get tired of this life. But everyone else does too, so I am not alone.

My folks are okay, I guess How are yours? Doing well, I hope.

I turned in for the allotment today. I hope you can get it now with no more bother. You will probably have someone come out to investigate to make sure all is hoyle. So, if they come, just answer what they ask you. Maybe they won't bother you at all.

I'm glad you got the gun. I hope the boys get as much good use as I did out of it. I have killed a lot of rabbits with it. I hope they do too. I would like to be there to help them. We shot a deer the other day so we had deer meat to eat. It was pretty good meat. There is a lot of deer and a few bears, too. But it is against the law to hunt them. We got the deer anyway. My sis said she could just feel a stomach kicking. That is funny. I never had a stomach kick me before. Haha. Don't take me wrong. I am only kidding you.

I am listening to the radio as I write this. We get the Grand Ole' Opry sometimes. Other times we can't pick it up. I wish I was there listening to the Grand Ole' Opry with you. I would be much happier. Do you think we would get much listening done?

Hey! Tell Bill the next time he is giving his wife a big kiss to think of me out here in the wilderness. I want to be giving a certain lady a big kiss, too. He sure is a lucky boy. Sometimes, I get very lonesome for someone. I can't be for sure what her name is but it runs in my mind like this . . . Cora Mae, I Love You.

Honey, if your allotment doesn't go through, at least you know I tried and did not let you down. We just have to trust in good luck. Tell the folks hello for me and tell me how you are getting along. I worry about you. I love you so much, I can't help worrying. Tell that old boyfriend of yours that if he messes around or cause you and me any trouble while I am in the army, I will treat him just like I would a Jap if I ever got the chance. I'll use my army bayonet on him. Haha. It is about one and a half foot long, three inches wide and sharp as a razor. It is used to cut people, if need be. You ought to see it. Isn't that some way for me to talk? Anyway that is the way I feel if he causes you any trouble.

Are you having any trouble with the fellows there? If so, let me know. I can't think of much more to write about and guess I had better close, but before I do, I want to say one thing. This is very important to me and you . . . I love you. Believe me?

So for now, I'll say goodnight and good luck,

Your husband, Charles

SWAK, SWAK, SWAK

To My Wife, The One I Love & Worship. Cora Mae I Love You.

To The Sweetest One I Know, Cora Mae
To My Darling Wife, Cora Mae,

Well, Honey it is Sunday and Valentine's Day. I didn't send a valentine to anyone, did you? I will send a picture as soon as I can.

The boys are talking about women. I wish you could be a mouse and hear it. They are talking about how they want their wives to be and what they would do if they should ever step out on them. Boy, they are going to treat them mean. I can just see that. I don't ever think of my wife stepping out. Do you think you will? Honey, that would make me unhappy. Would it you?

I haven't even talked to a woman since we were married. I am trying to live up to what we have promised each other. When I get to wanting a woman, I just think of you and I can't bear to think of doing you wrong. I always thought It would be hard for me to be true to one girl, but I don't notice it at all. I just got all my faith in you and I can't think of doing you wrong either. I have you to put my faith in. You don't know how much I look to you for love and how much love I get just in thinking of you. It is almost like worshiping God. I just get to thinking of you and it really makes me happy. That is what they really mean by real love.

I just rolled a cigarette. Would you like a puff of it? Have you been smoking lately? How are the children? Are they doing well? I hope so. Tell Bill if I were there I would give his wife a kiss. Would you let me? He would beat me with a club, I bet. No Honey, I wouldn't kiss anyone but my own sweet wife. I would be kissing you all the time. I would undress you. Unless, you got tired of it. I wish I was there to try and see if you would get tired of it.

Well, Darling, I will close, saying I love you. You can't imagine how much.

So Honey, Bye, Bye for now.

Your husband, Charles SWAK, SWAK I love you, honest I do.

To The One I Love, Cora Mae,

Again I am writing even though I have nothing to write about. Things are as usual here, very rainy. I received a box of candy for Valentine's Day. It had gone to the wrong address, but they sent it on to me. Aunt Agnes sent it.

Honey, I really didn't write a very good letter of answering your last letter, but I was in a stupor and couldn't think of much to say in answering it. But, you know I love you and as I told you many times forgive me for writing a poor letter once in awhile, won't you?

They are going to change me again and put me on day shift. I don't care where they put me just as long as time passes fast and gets me closer to the day I can be near you again. That is all I live for now and that is to come back to the one I love. You know who that is don't you? I wouldn't mention any names but her initials are CMW. You know her?

How is Odell making out on the draft? Has he been called yet? How is Robert and Jesse doing these days? I sure wish I was there. I would give you a good loving. Would you let me? I would probably do it anyway. I love you so dearly. I don't know what to do. Do you remember the letter when I said we would call it quits? I sure am glad we didn't. Aren't you? Well, I am sure glad we didn't. Aren't you? I'll say now in the way of apologizing, I am sorry I ever wrote that letter. Will you accept my apology?

You know when I didn't write for along time and finally wrote you? You said you had been dating an old boyfriend. That must have kind of woke me up. I knew in my heart then that I didn't want anyone else to have you. I guess I was jealous and I suppose I still am. You don't blame me do you?

I get to thinking of you and I working to make a life together and it makes me feel good all over. I use to work and things wouldn't work out, I wanted to just give up. I didn't have anyone to love me or give me a good reason to work for. I could only look forward to meeting someone and trying to make them. Now, I got you to look forward to and to try to make happy. I can work with more heart now that I know you care as much as I do. I am one hundred percent proud that you are my wife and no one can take you away from me. I know that God meant you or me and after fooling around for so long, I know now that I want you forever in my life and only you.

I can't think of much more to say, but always remember that I will always do everything I can to make you proud to be my wife and make you happy to be so. If we don't get a chance on earth to be with each other, I know we will be together in heaven. Because I know we will be together somehow.

So, Darling, give each of the children a kiss and hug from me. And tell Jr. just what I said about being good until we can all be together. The morning I left, I told him to be a good boy for his mother until I got back.

So Honey, for now, I will say so long and good luck. From one who will hold you dear to his heart, always,

Your husband, Charles SWAK

Dearest Cora Mae,

Well, Honey, I will try to write you now. Everything here is okay. Hope it is there, too. The weather is very nice and it makes me wonder how it is there. I just got done shaving and my face burns like fire. I guess I shaved too close.

Honey, I ain't got no mail from you in two days. I guess you are busy moving and all that. I hope when you get this you are done with it. I hope you will be content there. I am glad you are moving as it is time you have a place of your own. You are better off there. Your folks may not think so, though. I am not going to say I don't like it as I think it would be the best. I only wish I could be there with you. That sure would make me happy.

Honey, about that allotment, I can't let you know about it until I find out. The only way I am going to find out is when they take it out of my paycheck. If that does not happen this month, I am going to find out what is wrong. You see it means just as much to me as it does to you, because the longer it takes, it means that it is just that much longer it ain't getting to you. as I figured on. I will try to explain what I mean. The government pays me fifty dollars a week. When the allotment is okayed, the government will take twenty-two dollars out of my fifty and add twenty-eight dollars and send it to you. So you see, when the allotment goes through, that would mean that I am just losing twenty-two dollars. So you see the sooner things goes through, the better it will be for both of us. I hope it goes through soon.

Well, Honey, I can't think of much more to say, only that I love you. Tell the children I said hello. Also, your brothers, Bill and Jesse. Honey, how is Robert getting along? Tell all I said hello. I must close for now. Maybe I can think of more to say before I mail this. I am hoping for a letter from you tonight.

Well, Honey, I got your letter. Sure was glad to get it. I am glad you are okay and getting your house set up. I wish I was there to help you. Hey, you never said anything about you having cow to milk or a calf to feed. Did your Pa let you milk one or what?

Say, Honey, I wrote my folks about you coming up to Ohio to meet them. They said they would like for you to come but it would be better to wait until the weather got warm up there. Mom said May would be best weather. She said it was thirteen degrees below zero right now. But anytime you came it would be okay by them. So, Honey, if you want to go now, it is okay or if you want to wait until I get a furlough, that would be okay, if I happen to get one. I'll leave it up to you.

Well, Honey, I've got to get my washing done. I would make a good washerwoman, Haha. I'll bet I could be a good housekeeper, too. I would probably make you more dirt than three people could clean up.

There ain't much more I can write about, only how much I love you, more than anything else in this world. You can tell the world that your husband really loves you even if he can't be there with you. If I could hold you in my arms I would be happier than I am out here.

About going to the show, Honey, They are shown right here on the base. So I don't have to go off camp to see one. About that dancing, well if you can't learn me, maybe after the war is over, we can learn together then if you want to. I sure wish it would come soon as I sure am getting lonesome for you.

It has been six months since I last saw you. That sure is a long time. I only hope I don't have to serve that long again.

Well, Darling, for now I say Aloha and will go to bed. Tell everyone I said hello to them and good luck.

Darling always remember that I love you.

Your Husband, Charles SWAK SWAK SWAK

Grover Hill, Ohio
December, 21, 1942

Dear Daughter,

We were all surprised to receive your and Charles letter saying you had gotten married. Charles seems very happy in his letter so we are all glad he is satisfied. If you and Charles are satisfied that is all that matters as each one of us has to make our own decisions in this world. We will do all we can to make you happy.

We were surely surprised to learn that Charles had come east and hadn't stopped by in Ohio. I wrote him that maybe we could all meet here on his next furlough and get acquainted together. He could come here and you could come too. That way we could both be happy.

We got a letter from him today. He said he is expecting to be moved soon, so his furlough may be over. I hope he gets another before he leaves America. If he doesn't maybe you could come anyway. We are all just plain farmers here and Charles says your folks are farmers too, so we have something in common.

It is a real winter here this year. It was below zero last night. We have about six inches of snow and expect to get more. I imagine it gets cold there too but not quite as cold as it gets here.

Mom ordered your wedding present but it hasn't come yet. I apologized for not writing sooner but everything was so sudden and unexpected, we didn't hardly know what to do. Charles had never said a word. Mom said she would write when she sends your wedding present. Maybe we will get better acquainted by then as Charles said you folks might decide to come to Ohio after he gets out of the service.

Well I will close, wishing you both happiness and joy in your marriage. Please write as will be very happy to hear from you.

Be Happy,

Your new Father-in-law

1943

Dearest Cora Mae,

I received your letters with the pictures. Sure was glad to get them. Every letter I got I looked for them. I sure was proud of them too. I showed them to everyone who came into my tent.

You know dear, I can't think of much to say right now so I will finish this in the morning.

Well, it is the evening of the fifth now and I got your letter of New Year's Eve. You say you are lonely and want me very much. Honey, you can't want me any more than I want you. I long for you every day and wish we are able to be together at least for some of the time. Girl, don't think I wouldn't love to give you a bath if we could be together.

I would put you to bed, too, but you would have a bed partner. I would get in right with you. I will never forget sleeping with you. That is the nicest place to sleep I ever knew. Will I be happy if I could be with you now? You bet!! Don't think I am sex crazy when I talk of sleeping with you. I would be happy just sleeping in the same house with you. Any man would like that. I like your sex relations very much. But I love you for more than that. You are the nicest girl I ever knew. I know that I love you and am very proud of you. Honey I can't say what I want because I don't know how. The only thing I can say is that I love you for what you are and God must have put you on earth for me.

Please don't ever think I married you just so I could sleep with you for awhile. That was far from my mind. My heart is what made me marry you. I just kept saying I love her over and over again. I know I never would be satisfied without I had you as my wife. You believe me, don't you? Three short words "I love you" says it all.

You say you haven't had a letter from me for three days. I haven't missed over one day or two days writing to you since I came to Camp Ord. My letters must have gotten lost. I know it takes four to six days for yours to get to me and I know three days shouldn't pass without you getting one. I am going to send one page of your letter back to you so you could explain it to me. I can't make it out. I think I know what you mean, but I will underscore it.

I am trying to be as understanding and true to you in every way I can. I only want to understand you in every way I can. My only happiness in life is to do anything that will make you happy. Your name is Ward and I am very happy I was the one to make that your name. I will do all I can do to make you never be sorry for having that name. So keep your chin up and always a smile for me and be honest and true with me and I will never let you down. I would die first. I've got lots of faith and confidence in you and I have given you my life as you have given me yours. We can make one another's life very happy or unhappy. But I will never make you unhappy. I would rather die first.

So at this time, I will close as I got to be on guard at nine o'clock. So remember I love you and always will. Tell your folks I said hello and good luck. Tell the children I said hello and I send my love to them.

Your husband, C.W.Ward Please answer soon. SWAK XOXO

Dearest Darling Wife,
Cora Mae, I love You

Well, I will answer your letter. In the nicest way I can. You told me your ex-husband was hanging around, trying to make trouble for you. I hope someday he comes around when I am there. One of us would end up in a sad way. I told you once, I have no respect for a man like that. They haven't the right to be called a man. I really don't know how you want me to feel about him but the way I feel right now, it won't be good for him or I if we should ever meet. I can't help feeling the way I do because of the hurt he has caused you.

I won't tell you what to do about him. You can do whatever is right in your mind. The only thing I will say that if he is causing you trouble, he will pay for it to me in my own way when I get to see him. You know, the army teaches us to fight for keeps. But civilian law won't let you fight that way. I get so mad thinking of him. I only wish he was out here with me. He would soon be straightened out or crippled up. He needs to be where one has to back up what he says or does.

Honey, I may seem like an animal when I say things like this, but I can't help it. He messed up your life once. Now, you are mine, you and everything you stand for and your children also. You belong to me. If your ex husband ever tries to come between us, he will never live.

Well, I guess I ought to keep my mouth shut, but I just can't help it. I love you so much I can't bear to think he could hurt you again. I would never hurt you like he did.

Well, Darling, I am going to close so I can calm down and not say things I will be sorry afterward for. Remember I love you and our children. I will always take care of you if you will let me.

Forever and ever,
Your husband, Charles SWAK SWAK

1943

To the Swellest & Sweetest Wife a Man ever Had,
Cora Mae, I love You.

Well I got your letter of the sixth, the one with your mother's letter in it. I sure was glad to get it. Your mother is okay by me. Is she always like that? We will always be friends. Honey, I don't care for your folks to get me anything for Christmas. I just want to have your mother and dad to write me more often.

Honey, I love you so much I don't know how I am going to stand it until this war is over. You know I will never forget my promise to come back to you. I love you too much.

I know God will see to it that we will be back together. I don't go to church much but if you want me to, I will. I believe in Him. I always did believe in Him but not like I should. He will see us through this. Don't worry about me because I will get back okay. I just couldn't lose what I just found when you mean so much to me. I only live to be with you and that is the truth. I would be so happy if I could be with you now. Honey. I am getting tired of life in the army and only live anxiously to get back to you. One never knows how much they will miss someone until they to be away from them. And that is the truth.

You can bet your life that I will never leave you when I can come back to stay. I would give my right leg if I could hold you in my arms tonight. Boy, I sure would give you the best squeezing you ever got. You do believe me when I tell you these things because I have never been so in love in my life.

You are on my mind all the time. I dreamt we were together last night and it seemed like real life. It was so nice. I wish I could dream like that every night. It seemed so good to be near you but I am asking God to make it come through.

Honey, I am running low on conversation so I will close for this time.

Your Honey Forever,

C.W.Ward SWAK

Cora Mae, My Wife For Always,

Well we got our new address today. I will put it in this letter. You said you didn't get your present yet. If you haven't received it by the time you get this letter, you write and let me know. It might have got lost. If you didn't get it, I will send you another. Let me know if you got the money, too.

Honey, about those birth records, I didn't mean to make you think you had to make a special trip for them. It is that the quicker I get them the quicker the allotment will come through. I realize how it is and you can only go to town when you get the chance. I only want to so what you want me to do.

My Mom wrote and said she sent you a gift. I know when she meets you she will love you just as much as one of her own daughters.

Well, I got a haircut the other day and the barber made a miscut and cut my ears with his scissors. I told him that if he did that to my other ear I wouldn't pay him for the haircut. He said it was okay by him. But I still had to pay so maybe I will have better luck next time.

Well Honey you told me to believe in God so I guess I will. I think He will be the only One who can bring us together again. I will do anything in the world for that to happen. When I get out we will always be happy. I'll have a wife to kiss each morning and night. A wife who can make life worth smiling and a little one to adore at all times. Anything we can do to make our life complete and happy is what we will work for. All I look forward to now is my furlough or an armistice.

Well I need to close for now. Tell the children to be good for me and tell everyone hello. So long for now, as I've got to write to my folks and Sis. Honey when you get this I hope you will be as happy as I like for you to be. So bye.

There is no one who can take your place in my heart. I can only imagine what it would be like living with you all the time. If I ever get to, I will never leave you. I will always love you and trust you, no matter what happens or where we are.

So long again,

Your husband, Charles

SWAK

1943

Dearest Cora Mae,

I received your letter today and was proud to get it, as it is the only one I have gotten in three days.

I am glad all is okay there. My thumb is in pretty bad shape. They cut it open in two places. It hurt so bad I had to breathe from a bottle of smelling salts to keep from passing out. It hurts when I write, but I have put off writing to you for so long now. So don't worry if you don't hear from me for two or three days in a row as I ain't wrote you for nearly that long.

Honey, I am glad you have lots of hope for me. I have never told you anything that I did not want you to believe and will try to live up to until the day I die. I will also try to make your life a happy one. I know it will be hard on us. But I have always had to get things the hard way anyhow. I imagine you have too, so you won't be too surprised. I would hope to give you the world but I doubt that would happen. But as long as we try to get along, things will work out.

I'm sure glad O'dell is getting along well. How is Roy coming along? He and your other brothers treated me fine. You sure have a good family. If I could see you right now, I would be so happy.

Well Cora Mae, I must close as my thumb hurts.

Your husband, Charles

Grover Hill
January. 10, 1943

Dear Sis,

How is everything in your part of the country? Everything here is as usual, rain, ice, sleet & snow. There hasn't been any school here since they let out for Christmas. They will probably commence tomorrow.

Has there been any floods down there in Tennessee yet? A couple of times, the water in the bottom creek came up pretty high. But there hasn't been any damage yet. The rain and snow made the chores a lot more work. The cows get muddy and dirty and we have to bed down more cows to keep them cleaner and drier. About one more week and the haystack will be gone.

Did you receive the gun yet? I hope so. I hope whoever uses it has good luck with the gun. I always liked to use it to hunt with. It is solid built and in real good shape. You need to watch and be careful in handling so there won't be any accident.

I hear my uncle down in Payne has written you. Whatever you do, don't pay too much attention to him. For he has always been a great fella to razz someone. I don't know what he or his wife has wrote or razzed you about, but don't take it to heart, as he doesn't mean anything about it. But if you ever get up here and meet and spend time with him, you will know why I'm telling you this. Now don't think I am running him down or anything. He is alright. But he may say something that will hurt your feelings and not mean anything about it at all. And he wouldn't want to hurt Wes, or as you call him, Charles, to think you and he had gone wrong in getting married at all.

I know that if you and Wes wanted to come up here to live and couldn't find a place to move or stay, you would be most welcomed to his home to stay. And you would feel at home.

Well, I guess I had better sign off as it is getting bedtime.

So long and the best to you and Wes.

Your new brother in law & brother

Earl

To the One I Love, That is You
Cora Mae, I Love You.

Everything here is okay and it is a nice shiny day here for a change. I didn't receive no letter today but will probably get more tomorrow.

Now about this furlough business. I don't want you to count on it too strong because you know no one can ever be for sure. So, I say, don't be too sure until I know I get one for sure. Anything can happen these days and I don't want you to get yourself all built up and then you are in for a let down if I don't get it. If I don't get one, I am going to be a very disappointed boy.

Honey, how is everything down there? Okay I hope. My finger is coming along okay. It healed fast. I guess I am going to have to be very careful around knives. When you asked me about sitting under that tree, did you mean the one we sat under the Sunday I was heading for home? Or the one we sat under the day we got married? I wasn't mad at anything or anyone either time. I can't blame you for not letting me do what I wanted to do before we got married and it was better that waited until we got married. Did you want me to say I was sorry for what I did and how I acted before we got married? But Honey, I am glad things turned out as they did because I got me a wife that I love more than anything in the world. And if I had got what I wanted before we got married I would have thought you were a vain and lazy girl. And I did learned how much I loved you. So you see Darling, I am glad it turned out like it did. I never will be sorry of my bargain and I hope you won't. I believe I got as nice a wife as a man could have.

I got all my faith and hope in you and I will always have faith in you. So, lets both put our trust in God and hope for the best. Some folks might think we won't get along when we are living together, but Honey, we can prove they are wrong can't we? We can just love and be true to each other because if I were to lose you, I would dream about you all the time. I can still feel the nearness of you from the week we spent together. It was the best week I ever spent.

Well, I will close for now and say so long. I'll try to write some tomorrow. I hope I can see you soon.

With Love,

Your husband, Charles

XOXOXO SWAK

To the Swellest Wife a guy ever had,
Cora Mae I Love You,

I received two of your letters today. You asked what SWAK means. It means Sealed With A Kiss. If nothing happens, my address will change again for about eight weeks. They are going to send me to Bakers & Cooks school.

You said you hoped I wouldn't get mad at the way you talk in your letters. The only thing that would make me mad is for you to quit talking that way. We are man and wife so it is okay for us to talk any way we please.

I am glad Robert did not pass his examination. He is a lucky boy. Tell him he never will regret not going into the army. It is a hard life and full of different kinds of trouble.

Don't you ever think I get tired of your letters. I look forward to them very much. I am glad you got the pictures. I am on one of the horses. My horse was acting up and jarred my helmet off my head. You can do whatever you please with them. I want you to have all my pictures so you can't forget me.

I wish I was there to sit around the fire with both you and the children. We sure would be happy if I were to sleep there with you and keep you warm. It would be good. I don't have to guess, it would be good. It would be the nicest thing I ever had the pleasure of doing. Do you think I could keep you warm if I were there?

Well things ain't changed much here and news is scarce so outside of answering your letters, I can't think of much to write about. Remember I will always love you. So be good and I will do the same for you. Explain where I drew the line. I don't get the meaning of it. Maybe, I am just dumb but I don't know what "hay shuck" means.

So, Darling, I love you more than anything in the world. Believe in me because that is the truth. Tell our children I send my love. And Honey, even if you are as big as I am, I would still spank you, if you needed it. Haha

Tell your mother that I will get you and her one of those pillow cases that has a verse on it. They are hard to get though. So, Honey, since it is late, I will close. Tell all I said hello and I wish them good luck.

Your husband, Charles SWAK

P.S. I know what hay means but what does shuck mean? Do you mean corn shuck? I am slow to get it I guess. If God will bring us back together, I will be a good boy for the rest of our life and go to church every chance I get.

1943

Dear Son & Daughter,

Decided to write you a letter to let you know I am still kicking. Kenny caught three fox squirrels and is he ever puffed up.

Everything here is coming along. The popcorn looks as if it will make one half ton per acre or more. The beans are mostly safe from frost. We have seventy acres that are shedding their leaves. They look to need another week and a half until we can start harvesting. We have seventeen acres of wheat and eight acres of rye sowed and most of the manure hauled. We are going to put a cement platform on the east side of the barn like the one on the south end.

Ken has one hundred twenty five red rock hens that are laying eighty eggs a day. Mom and Alice sold their chicks. It brought them over a hundred dollars all told. We sold our fat hogs last week. They brought three hundred fifty dollars. We have two to butcher.

We went to the fair one day last week. It was real cold. We heard from Earl. He sent a picture and he is looking good. We haven't heard from Jim yet. There was a mock funeral for Leon Miller last Sunday. He got killed at Maunda. He was Orpha's brother. Two of Bill Harshman's boys got wounded over there too.

We mowed hay today and the clover is heavy. Tomorrow, Kenny and I will take it in. Dan goes to school and Bob Ross got a new tractor. He was sowing wheat today with it. He sold his eleven twenty tractor last fall and didn't try to farm. He just milked his cows.

Dan and Alice are growing like pigs. Dan is as tall as I am now. He was squirrel hunting the first day and came in about noon and said there just wasn't any squirrels this year. We have had several messes since then. Old John doesn't come to hunt any more so that leaves more for us. I bought two bushels of tomatoes for Mom today. That means tomato soup this winter.

Hope you get a furlough this fall and can come home. I get homesick to see you. Sure keeps us busy this fall since Earl pulled out but next year we will just farm this and can handle it better. We had thirty four pigs but we want to sell twenty of them so we don't have to winter them. We will keep two sows for next spring.

Mary and Irene came out this noon. Mom and they went up to see Zelma's mother this afternoon. Irene is married now and lives in a trailer down by Dayton. She says she likes it just fine. Wilbur is still at Camp Perry and gets home every Sunday. Carl Shelnebucker is married. What do you think of that? He married some girl from Paulding.

Well, Mom says she is going to bed so I will close and go to bed too. I hope we'll get to see you and Cora this fall. George Lulf's wife is very sick. She has cancer and can't get over it. The doctor says it will only be a few days. Charlie and Mike are both in the army. It will leave George all alone. That is tough luck. George is a pretty good neighbor, too. Bill Scherer is somewhere over in Italy, in the Seventh Army.

Well, will close,
Dad

To My Dearest Wife, Cora Mae,

I'll bet you are surprised to get two letters from me in one day, as I mailed one out at two o'clock. Also. I got your letter today so I will answer that one too. It is about eight thirty in the evening.

You said you got a letter from my brother. I am glad he wrote you. Mt folks will get over their hurt. They can't help feeling bad as I am the only one of their boys to get married so far. The one who wrote you is a twenty-eight years old and hasn't thought of marriage yet, I don't think. But he will find the right one someday as I did. I only hope he gets as nice a one as the one I got. He is right when he said we would get along if we pull together.

I got a letter from Sis today. She wishes us lots of luck and happiness. So, Honey, two of my folks are for you, so far and the rest will come around when they realize that we got married because we love each other and because of what some other things that might cause young people get married at the wrong time. We will prove ourselves to our family, no matter how hard it is for us. Don't you think we can?

I am glad your folks have some good hopes for me because I want them to know that I really love their daughter and have respect for her.

Honey, you said you haven't been getting any mail. I have wrote you every day except two and they were six days apart, if I remember right. So, maybe they aren't reaching you. You asked if they found out we were married. Honey, the army requires you to report it if you get married while on furlough. So you see, Honey, they knew as soon as I reported back for duty.

Did you get my letter asking you to get a duplicate of our marriage license and send that to me. If you didn't, when you get to town, would you do that for me? I will need it to put in for an allotment for you and the three children. You will have to get a judge or notary public to do it. If it is too much trouble, you can send the license out here to me and I will do it. It may be easier if I get on of the camp's notary public to do it. You can do either one you want. It will be alright by me.

You don't need to worry about me not letting your folks down either. I will always do right by you no matter what happens. We won't let neighbors nose in on our private lives, either. And I think we both know that anyway. I never did like anyone who spreads gossip. That is the root of evil.

Well, Honey, I will close for now, so I bid you adieux for now or goodbye.

From your loving husband

1943

To The One I Love,

Well Honey, I received your letter today. I am glad you are okay.

Honey, about the children going to see their grandma. Now it wouldn't be so bad but it is like you say. Their daddy will be there too. Then that is different. It is just like I said before. I don't want anything to do with your ex, so the children will stay home. I know they would like to see their grandma but if she wants to see them then she can come stay with you for awhile. I don't want them around their daddy, so if you don't mind if she stays with you, then it would be okay. Otherwise it won't be.

I would most likely ask you the same thing again if we were under that tree. If I get a furlough again, I will come there first so we could spend a awhile under that tree again. Also I am anxious to spend some time in our home as anyone can be, so darling I can't wait for my furlough. It looks like I will be stationed someplace near the Mexican border as my name was picked. If we do go, I will be a sergeant again. But I am afraid if I go I will lose my furlough. So I hope I won't go because I do not want to lose that furlough for anything.

I ain't wrote for nearly a week now as I don't have much time. I also had a real bad cold. I will try to do better someway.

Honey, the reason I want you to meet me halfway to see my folks is because for me to come there and then go to Ohio to see my folks will cost just that much more money. But if you say to come there then I will come there. So we will look at it that way and do it that way so we can be back there under that tree. Honey, you can bet I would like to be there again. But most of all, I would just like to have you back in my arms. I can't think of anything nicer . . . can you?

Well, I've got to take instructions on machine guns so I had better close for now.

Well, I am back now as I got the machine gun all oiled up. What a machine gun got to do with cooking is something I don't understand.

I need to go take a shower and get ready to do the cooking tomorrow. Say hello to everyone for me and tell the boys hello also. I'll say so long for now. I love you and will say adios.

I LOVE YOU.

Your husband, Charles SWAK

To The One I Love, Cora Mae,

Well I received your letter today and was very glad to get it. Honey, I am glad you got the money before Christmas. Don't think about paying me back. If I send something to you then it is yours. You don't spend my money. You spend our money and that is the way I want it to be. When I send money then it is yours. The only thing that isn't yours is you because you are mine now. I don't even think of anyone else getting you. Whatever you do is for the best so don't worry over me being mad.

Honey, send those birth certificates, as I will need them. It will be for the best of all if I get them soon. I know it seems slow, but things like that takes time. But it will be worth it in the long run as it will mean more money for you and the children. I hope you got your present. Your letters are still coming, but addressed to Camp Young. I hope you got my letters with the new address on it.

Darling, do you think your brother will be called soon. I hope not as it can be awful hard on a person. You know, Honey, our mail has been twice as long reaching each other but maybe it will be more on time at this camp. It looks as though we will be at Camp Ord for awhile yet so send your mail to me here. I can't think of much to say except I love you and can always say that, don't you think? Haha

Honey, I was glad to get the letter from your Mom. I'll bet if I was to take that belt and hit your daddy, he would have given me a whipping too. Haha. Don't you think so? Tell him I don't hold any hurt over it. I know he didn't mean it. But if I ever mistreat his daughter I want him to whip me and I will offer no resistance whatsoever. If anyone ever mistreat a girl of ours I would fight them every time I saw them.*

---

* Mom swore her father had never lifted his hand to her before. Grandpa was so upset that Mom had married someone that he almost considered a foreigner and feared he would take Mom and we children back to Ohio that his heart was broken. When Mom accused my brother of lying to her about playing with matches and spanked him, Grandpa lost it and whipped Mom with the same belt. Mom and Dad went down to stay at her brother's place then and Grandma came over and begged Mom to come back to talk with Grandpa as he was beside himself with regret. Mom had been through some hard times during her divorce and Grandpa had stepped in and took care of all of us. He feared the same could happen again and he wouldn't be close to help. His nerves just got the best of him as he was the gentlest man I ever knew.

Honey, please believe me when I say I love you and proud to have you as his wife.

From one who worships you. I do, so help me God. Answer soon.

Your husband, Charles XOXO

Honey, don't forget to send me their birth records as soon as you can. The sooner I turn them in the quicker you will get the allotment. The army is slow in something like that.

1943

To Cora Mae, The One I Love,

Well, I guess by now you will have thought I have deserted you. But I just couldn't get time to write. I was out in the woods for four days and it rained everyday. I am working in the kitchen again. We sure are having our share of rain, now.

Honey. I got all your letters and will try to answer them all right away. You know whatever you will do is alright by me, just as long as it is for the best and is right. I got your Mother's letter and was glad to get it. Honey, if you go to see my folks, you know I will be thinking of you all the time, wishing I could be with you, if you go. I guess my folks would like very much for me to come back and farm for them. You and I can decide on that when we get back together again.

When you write to me, you can write all the foolishment you want. I like to hear your letters that way. It makes me feel as if we really believe and trust in one another. When we write about those days we spent together, we should not be ashamed of anything. We can talk freely about anything because we are first, one and the same. You don't need to worry about how I feel about your foolish talk because if you didn't talk that way, I would think you didn't love me. I am glad you do talk that way.

Well, Darling, are you living by yourself now? How are you getting along? How is our family? I sure wish I could be there with you and them. We would be very happy together. We would sure enjoy our life.

Well, I can't think of much to say right now. I can write everyday now if we don't happen to move again or I am sent out on patrol again. You know I will write every chance I get. Boy, Darling, I could use on of your rib tickling.

The mess sergeant just came in and gave me your letter with the marriage certificate and birth certificates. I guess I can get along without the other records. I hope so anyway. I will let you know how I make out. I will take good care of these records and our marriage license. I will send them back as soon as I can.

But for now, Darling, I love you. Keep hoping and praying and I will do the same. I couldn't get mad over that word you wrote on the envelope. I just didn't know what it meant.

Tell all I said hello and good luck. From the one who is awful lonesome for you, Charles

1943

To The Sweetest Girl I Know,
Darling I Love You,

Well Honey another day has gone by. They are having a dance in camp tonight. I can't dance but if you were here we could learn to dance. If nothing happens my address will change in a week. I hope so anyway. Some of the boys went on their furlough today. I sure wish I was leaving on mine.

I went to the dentist to get my teeth cleaned today. She done a good job. She cut my gums a little but not too much. There is something I have to talk over with you when I come home. To see if there is some way for you to come out here. So we could spend more time together than just my furloughs. I thought we might arrange it for you to come out here to live with me for a while. Let me know if you think we should try anything like that. I want your honest opinion on it. It is a long way from Tennessee.

Well Honey, I can't think of much else to say. Honest, I love you more than anything in this world. Tell the children I send them my love. So I'll say so long for now. Say hello to all your folks. Darling I love you. Do you think I could talk you into marrying me? Again, I mean. Haha. I could use a girl just like you for my wife. Don't mind me. I get that way sometime.

Your husband,

Charles

Dearest Wife,
Cora Mae, I Love You,

Honey I got two letters from you today. One from the 6th and one from the 8th . . . Sure glad to get them. I also got a letter from Odell and his wife. He said you all were done with the tobacco. I'll bet you were good at that. I wish I was there to help Bill cut cord wood. And then I could be there with you at night.

I'm glad Jr. is in school and doing good because he will be proud in later years. I would have gone further if I had. If I live to be the children's father, I will see to it they get as much education as they want.

I was fixing to go to the show but got your letter and thought I would get more pleasure answering it. About the question you asked me. If I ever need money, I will let you know. About the only time would be for a furlough. Otherwise, if I go broke, I will go without until pay day. I figure like this. My wants are many but my needs are few. I find out I can do with less money than I thought I could. You see, Honey, I have put all my faith and trust in you for all my present and future happiness. If I send all the money I can, you will save all you can. What you save will be just that much we will have when we are together. Honey, what is mine is yours. What is yours is mine. Doesn't that seem right? So, I trust in you to do as you think best. If you need money, just go right ahead. You don't have to ask me. And if I need money for my furlough, I will write and tell you and you can send it to me. Or if you don't happen to have it, then I will do the next best thing. As long as you think best, it will be alright.

I wish I could see Betty in her new outfit. You said she was sore on her setter. Did she get rid of that sore when I was there? About that cake, I ain't got it yet. I guess it got lost. I sure appreciate your kindness and I hope you don't think I would laugh or make fun of you unless I am teasing or something like that.

The pictures didn't come. I won't say anything to your mom because I don't want my wife choked. I sure wish I could be there to have dinner with you and your folks. I get tired of my own fixings.

I bet if I were there, I could see your legs even if you did have slacks on underneath. Haha. I wish I could see them nude. Well I would not object if you took my shorts off, even if you did tear them. I am still yours as you asked me to. Remember? And Honey I always will be. Honey, I like to hear you talk foolish. It doesn't sound foolish to me. With all of my heart, there is no use denying that I want all your passes and your love. Your passes are wonderful to me. I was afraid that one of us would not be satisfied with our sexual relations. But I am more than satisfied with yours. And I hope you are too because it helps to make our love inseparable and undivided. You can be sure that I won't ever give my love to any other as long as I have you. Those are the truest words I have ever spoken.

So I will close for now. I hope this finds you all well and happy. If I have said anything that might offend you, let me know so I can correct it. Tell all the folks hello and give my love to the children.

Your Husband,

C.W.Ward I love You, I Love You SWAK

In answer to your second letter, I hope by now your headache is long gone before you get this. I wish I could be there to hold you in my arms until it went away. I don't think it's funny for you to worship the shirt I got for you. I look at the little flowers you gave me. I look at it often and tell it how much I love the one who gave it to me. XOXO

March 20, 1943

Cora Mae, I Love You,

I received your letter today and was glad to get it. Honey I won't talk like that any more. I got a hearing for that allotment today that got all the way to the head office of New Jersey. They said I would receive notification when final action is taken on it. I was much relieved because I was afraid it may have gotten lost. If you hear anything of it, let me know.

What was I suppose to find out in the letter that you wrote this morning? I haven't received it yet. What was it? But don't you worry about it. Honey, no one but you can destroy my love for you. Troubles have always been knocking at my door. I am getting use to it by now. If you always play fair with me, we will be alright. Honey, everyone has their troubles. But things will always come out right if we are good and honest with each other.

Back to the question I asked you awhile back in another letter about the difference between an elephant and a bag of peanuts. Well . . . if you don't know the difference I would hate to send you a bag of peanuts. You might bring back an elephant. Haha.

Honey, tell the boys I said hello and wish the best for them. I haven't heard from my folks or my sis either. I would like to be there now. I would be so happy. Honey, I would marry your grandmother just to be in the same family with you. Have you ever seen anyone dumber than me. I just can't help it. I was born that way, I guess. You got to overlook me. I guess I never had a good reason to be smart. I just grew up in a hurry but I try to be a good boy.

How are you getting along? Do you like where you live now? Honey about that being hot and cold. A man is a fool, always wanting it to be cool when it is hot and always wanting it to be hot when it's not. That is a verse I heard some man say and just wrote it to you. It could mean several things but I like it the way it is. Haha. Don't get me wrong.

Honey, how is Odell and the draft coming along? I can't think of much more to say. But Darling, remember that no matter what happens, I am the one who will always love you.
Honey I mean well with all my heart.

The Grand Ole Opry is on and Earnest Tubb is singing, "Waltz Across Texas". That is my girl he is singing about. It sure makes me long for you. Hope you are listening to it as well. I've always wanted to go to the Grand Ole Opry. I have never had the chance yet. We will go together when I am there if I ever get another furlough. We will be happy one of these days.

About those people who want my address. You go right ahead and let them have it. Maybe if they write me I can write back and set things straight about how things are between you and me, as far as other people are concerned. They can't say anything to spoil my love for you. I won't believe it.

Well. Honey, I'll say adios for now and good luck. Give my love to our children. Say hello to everyone else, too. Honey as sure as I am writing this letter, I hope if I can't say I love you and mean it, I won't see daylight again. That is how sure I am that I love you. Just remember, I am all for you and depend on you for our future happiness and contentment.

From one who loves you dearly,

Charles Answer soon SWAK

I sure wish I were there to take your pants off. But for more reasons than that, haha. I would probably make love to you.

1943

To The Sweetest Girl I Know,
Dearest Cora Mae, My Wife,

Well Darling, I received your letters today . . . all four of them. It took them a long time to come from the cooking school.

Now about your hair. I will try to explain what I mean. I like your hair whether it is short or long. Anyway you want it. It will be a lot more comfortable for you, especially with the hot weather. So if you want it cut get it cut. Just as you like it.

Honey, I got your letter of the fourteenth, the one with your new address. I am glad you are okay. I will probably be needing some of your money for my furlough when I get it. I hope it will be soon.

I am going to answer those four letters in this letter. So here goes. I wrote that colored woman a letter. I don't have anything against colored people. They can't help they are colored. I am glad you got a letter from my mother. I am also glad you got the money order. All I can say is that I will play fair with you just as you play fair with me. And I trust you to always do that. As long as I have you and your trust is all that I need for myself. You never need worry about repaying me. You just be my wife and let me love you is all I ask. When you and I get together I will learn to love you even more than I love you now. And that is more than I can say.

You can get a tombstone for Shirley as that would be best. You can always find the grave as time goes on. In time, graves are left to waste. But if there is a tombstone, you can always find it. It is sure okay by me to get one for her.

I don't think I could ever get tired of my honey if you were the one I was getting it from. I sure would like to be getting some now. Wouldn't you?

Don't worry about the barber. She didn't cut too much off. Haha. Tell Bill & Polly I am very happy for them. They will be happy to have a little one to take care of. Maybe someday we will have little ones if that is okay by you. Is it? Honey you know I will take your pants off when I get home and I may be in too much of a hurry and not wait until we get to bed. I don't think you will have to do it for me. Tell Bill and Polly it ain't worth taking his pants off if he can't have it. Haha. I'll be he will take her pants off then. Haha.

Honey, you don't need to worry about how I feel about you going to that colored woman for advice or how I feel about that money. Honey, as long as you do right by me.

About your step-ins . . . Honey, I ain't seen them. That is a funny thing to lose . . . although I've heard of people losing their teeth. But if I see them anywhere, I'll be sure and let you know. I'm sorry, but I am laughing as I answer this. I can only wish. I wouldn't want your step-ins up all the time anyway. You know I wouldn't, don't you? So if any I send you don't fit, maybe you could exchange them.

Honey, I don't think it is wrong what we say as long as we think the same thing. We both love one another and like to be with each other for more reasons than one. So it can't be wrong as long as we love one another. Honey, we are man and woman and it is only human nature, so it can't be wrong. And we have that right now and no one can say anything about it. And God knows I want your love. So when we are together, you can bet someone's step-ins are going to be taken off. Maybe you know whose that will be. Haha. Hope you don't mind. Haha.

I wish I could be there to help you make garden. Think if I were to plant something it would grow? I remember a certain thing one week but I don't think it grew anything. Maybe it will next time. Haha.

Well, Honey, I have about ran out of things to say. I wish I were there to take your step-ins down and also to hold you in my arms again and give you a kiss.

Tell our children I send them my love.

Your husband, Charles SWAK I LOVE YOU

To the one I Love, Cora Mae,

Well just a line to let you know I am thinking of you. It is raining. I hope it isn't that way there. I signed the payroll again and they haven't started taking out the allotment yet. I don't know what is wrong. There is a knot in the rope somewhere and I am going to find it. I am getting tired of waiting for it to go through.

How are you getting along with your cow and calf? How are the boys doing? I bet they cut up like yearling colts. I wish I were there to do some cutting up with you. Say, do you know the difference between a Jap and a corset? Well, it takes a yank to take them both down.

I can't think of much to say. How are your folks? Do you like your new home? Have you had any spankings lately? I wish I was there to give you one.

I am writing this while I am waiting for dinner to be served. I ain't suppose to be doing it but I ain't got nothing else to do until then. I'll bet you will have a hard time making this out.

Tell the boys I said hello and I think of them a lot. When you put that slip on again, think of me and how I long to be there to help you put it on. Or "off" as the case may be maybe.

Honey, we have promised not to let what other people say cause problems between us. I still want that promise to be held by both of us. Please remember I love you with all my heart and soul. I always will. Let's keep it that way. What do you say? Do we forget our past and start over just like we were when we were born? I got your story and why you were divorced and I took your word for it. I've never thought different about you and never will. I married you for my wife and as long as you are a good wife, I promise I will always be a good husband and love you forever. Darling, you don't need to worry over me ever rejoining the army once I am out. I will be with you for always. I never will go off from you again.

You said you wonder sometimes how your ex done you and what I done. You say there is so much difference. You ask if I was dissatisfied, would I walk off and hurt you? Before I would hurt you or be dissatisfied, I would tell you and we could always come to a better way of settling it than by being separated. I am going to be truthful to you always and now I want you to answer this question. You are afraid I am going to become dissatisfied with our sexual relations. Am I right? Honey, I don't want you to take offense of this, but this is what I want you to do. You've got to promise me that you will never again worry about that. Will you promise me that? Give me an honest answer to my question. I love you so much that all I want to do is be with you when this war is over.

For now, I'll just say so long and good luck.

Your husband, Charles

P.S. Got your letter of the 14th and the 15th. I am glad you are okay. After I read those letters, I could have kilt someone. When people try to make trouble for you and I, they had better stay on their side of the fence. I would believe you before anyone else. People who try to mess me up had better keep away.

Darling, you know if we do each other wrong, it will come out in the end. Maybe your other husband did get tired of you. But, Darling I promise you I won't. You just go right ahead and give my address to anyone who wants it. Anything they write won't be held against anybody except the one who writes it. They ain't going to make me believe anything. The only one who can make me believe anything is you making me believe it. I've told you before what other people think, it don't worry me. All I want is you and your love. If other people try to make me think otherwise had better lay off. Lots of people will think I am a fool. Well, it won't hurt anybody if all they do is think it. Don't worry about me not believing you. They are just all troublemakers.

Honey, tell Polly I wish I were there taking off my shoes off on the bed.

Well, keep your chin up and don't pay no mind what people say and we will always be happy. So long for now From the one who loves and adores you. Please don't worry. Only you can stop me loving you.

Charles XOXOXO

1943

To My Dearest Sweetheart,
My Darling Wife, Cora Mae

I received your letter of the 22nd and you asked me why I haven't been writing you. By the time you get this you will know why. It took two days to get here and as soon as we got here, we went off on a four day patrol. I knew it would leave you wondering what was wrong, but it couldn't be helped. I hope you won't be mad at me over it, because I couldn't help it.

Honey, don't worry about anything you might write me would hurt me. The only thing you could say that would hurt me would be if you wrote and said you didn't love me and that would hurt me very bad. I hope you will never say that.

I am sorry you are not feeling well. Now you take care of yourself. I wish I could be there helping to strip the tobacco so you could do for me like a wife does when a husband can be with her supporting her like he should be. I know it is hard me being away like this. When I can be with you, I will never leave you alone. I will make you go with me wherever I go, even outside. All joking aside, I'll never go off and leave you alone as long as I can get you to go with me. You will never have to worry about me getting ready to go home when we go to town. I promise you will never have to sit and wait for me to go home like I have seen other men do their wives. Honey, you don't ever have to worry about me doing that way, as that is a mean way to be.

One of the boys came in to borrow my soap. You remember that soapbox you gave me? I use it everyday and think of you when I do. I never have been able to get someone who can cut your name in metal on it. You said you ran out ink. I don't care if you use charcoal, as long as you write.

I remember promising to come back to you no matter what happens. I am going to try to come back to you like the same guy I was before. I pray to God I won't come back otherwise. If my being with you and loving you well would make you well, you would be well in a hurry. You be careful and not get sick as I worry over you.

I am glad Bill's tobacco sold well. I guess I am going to cook and baker's school soon. I will send you my new address as soon as I find out myself. If you need money while we are waiting for the allotment, let me know. And I will try to send you some. You needn't worry about spending my or your money because it is okay if it takes it all, as long as I have you for my wife. All I can do won't repay you for the love you give me. Nothing matters as long as we are happy and I am happy just knowing you love me. I ask God every night to bring us back together and with our children. I also ask for a peaceful and happy life together. Honey, I believe He will do us that favor because He has been good to us so far. And if we both be good, I believe all will end good. I never said a prayer until you asked me to. I guess I have been a Baaaad Boy! But Honey, I won't be anymore. All I ask Him is to let me be with you and to love and make you happy. I haven't had much chance to make you happy while I have been in the army, but when I get out of here, I will do anything just to make you smile and love me.

We talked to each other about our passes and other things. Well, that just goes to show we love one another. We must always remember Who made that possible and not forget to respect and appreciate Him for what He has done for us. When we talk to one another, let's be truthful and openly free with one another. Don't hide anything from ourselves, as we are now man and wife. So don't think I will be mad when you talk of it.

Tell the folks I said hello. Tell Bill & Polly I said hello. Boy, I am glad for Robert not passing. He can say he is lucky. The army is a great thing but not for me. I know where I want to be and that is by your side.

So I must close for now,
Your loving husband, Charles SWAK

1943

My Dearest Wife, Cora Mae,

Well, Darling, here I am again and just pining away for you. I keep thinking about when I was there last time. I knocked on the door and there you were, in a red dress that buttoned down the front. But some of the buttons were opened near the bottom because you said you had been cracking walnuts on the hearth for the children. You said the rest of the family had gone to town to see a show. And since the car was full, you and the kids had to stay home. Even though you said you had been blue staying home, it sure was lucky for us both in the end. I had wanted to surprise you but if you hadn't been there I would have been the one surprised to have to had to wait until you got home. I guess God is looking out for us in some way.

Getting back to that red dress, I don't mind seeing a pretty leg if it is yours. I saw it that one time and would like to see more of it. Don't get me wrong but with my being away from you so long and just coming up and seeing your leg like that was a surprise for me. But I will say I liked it very much. You can't blame me can you? So try to have on a dress that opens in the front again so I can see it again. Haha

Honey, I don't know what you mean by "shuck out hay". Anyhow, I wish I were there so we could enjoy our passes together as we did before. I sure do think you are the best woman there ever was. I am very satisfied in that part. I would probably try to pull your pants off too. You wouldn't need to tell me to neither, I bet.

Honey, I hope it is okay by you if I answer like this. Just let me know if you like for me to write like this. Tell Bill the next time he takes Polly's pants off for some unknown reason, to think of me. Haha. I am only kidding. Write all the foolishness you can think of and I will answer it because we love each other and are married and it is our own business how we talk to each other.

I am glad my brother wrote you. He is a pretty good fellow. Just another "Ward" boy. You will find they are a pain in the neck. Just wait until we live together for fifty years and you will see. I hope we both live that long, don't you? But we will be happy no matter how long we live.

Well, things ain't much changed here and news is scarce. So outside of answering your letter, I can't think of more to write about. But no matters what happens, I will love you and always will. So be good and I will do the same. But write and tell me what "shuck hay" means. Don't be afraid to explain it. Maybe I am dumb.

Darling, keep your chin up and always remember that I love you more than anything in the world. That is the truth so please believe in me. Send the children my love. And even if you are as big as I am, I will spank you, if you need it. I love you.

Your Devoted Husband, Charles SWAK

1943

Dearest Cora Mae,

I received your letter and was very glad to get it. You took me wrong in my letter. I trust you and always will. I was mad when I wrote the letter but I didn't like when your ex was trying to cause you trouble. If I was ever there when he comes and cause you trouble, he won't ever bother you afterwards. But my hands won't always be tied up like they are now. His day is coming. But don't think what he says and does not make any diff to me because as long as you are true to me, no one will ever get the chance to cause us trouble.

I love you too much to let that happen. There isn't anything I believe in more than I do you. You know I had to love and believe in you very much because when we were married, we promised our lives to each other. If I had thought you would ruin my life then, I would not have married you. But I believed you were the one to make my life happy and I still believe that way. You are the one who has made my life happy so far. And my heart tells me you always will.

So don't worry about me not believing in you. I am only sorry we didn't get married the first day we met. But we will always be happy when we do get together. God has had our lives all planned out. Don't you think? If I hadn't been in the army, then we would never had met. And you would have been with someone else, so this is the way it was planned for us. With the will of God, all people's lives are planned the same way. He is the one who makes our lives go along as they do. I am sure your and my lives will be happy, once this war is over.

And about that spanking. Turn about is fair play. Don't worry about me beating you when you talk sassy to me. I wouldn't do anything like that. I might make you eat a little crow. Haha. I like for you to be sassy when you got a reason to be. Anyone who can live with a guy like me has a right to get sassy. Don't you think?

The guys see me writing so often they kid me. But I don't care as long as they don't say anything about you. Their time is coming. They will find the right girl sometime and I will kid them.

Well, Honey, I am going to close for now. You might not get your Christmas gift on time as I am very nearly broke. I left some of my pay out and sent it to you. I hope this finds you well and happy. It leaves me well but very lonesome.

Give your folks my best regards and to write a few lines in your letters every once in awhile. Tell your mother that if her daughter misbehaves, she should give her a licking. Haha.

Well hope to receive your letter with a big red kiss on it. Please believe me when I say I love you.

Your husband, Charles SWAK

To My Dearest Wife, Cora Mae,

Well, Honey, just a few lines to let you know I am okay. I got an infection in my thumb someway and it had been giving me some trouble. I got it all wrapped up and it should be okay in a day or so.

I am looking for a letter from you everyday now. Write as often as you can and I will do the same. You don't know how I wish this war could be over. I have so much to look forward to now. I didn't know life could mean so much. Being with you for a week sure changed my ideas about life a lot. I didn't know I could care so much for one person. The Lord will surely bring us back together and keep us there. Before, I never cared where I was or where they sent me. But now I only want to be one place and that is as close to you as I can get. I know that someday, not too far away, that I will be there with you.

I hope you can read this what with my sore thumb.

Write and let me know how your folks' crops are doing. How are the boys getting along? You sure have a nice bunch of brothers. They must think I am a funny guy but that is the way I am. I guess as long as you and I get along good, they will overlook my funny ways.

Honey, we will get along if we can possibly make it that way. I know you will do your part. A fellow doesn't know how he loves someone until he has to leave her.

I can't think of much more to write now and it is just about time for lights to go out.

Tell your folks or brothers to write a note on one of your letters once in awhile. Tell Odell to write too and tell his wife I said hello. Tell your brother Jesse to take it easy on those girls of his. Tell Robert to think of me when he checks his fox traps. How did he come out with his medical exam? Did he pass it? Please write to me often. Give the children a kiss for me.

Well, I've got to close. For now and always I will always love you.

Your husband, C.W. Ward SWAK

To The One I Love, Cora Mae, I Love You,

Honey, I guess I had better write, as I didn't get to write yet today. I got four letters from you today, though.

Honey, about the children going to see their grandmother. Now it is okay by me if they go there as long as she takes the right care of them and bring them back home when it is time for them to be back home. She can have them like that. But if there is any trouble, she can never have them again. Tell her it is okay by me but if there is any trouble, she won't get them anymore. I only want to be fair to everyone and if you think it is alright and you want them to go, it is alright by me. Just so no trouble comes of it.

Tell your folks I will answer their letter soon. I got one from my folks, too, that I need to answer.

I remember all about when we sat under that tree. All I can say is that someone was too anxious and you can guess who I mean. It didn't make me mad. You don't need to worry about making me mad at you and not letting you know of it. Cause Honey, when I get mad at you, you won't have any trouble knowing it, if you know what I mean. I don't believe I could get mad at you. I try not to, anyway.

When I get my furlough, I think it would be best if we met at my folks. I should be getting my furlough soon, about two or three months I should think. When I know for sure, I will let you know. You will have to send me money. Send it by telegraph or money order. You never did tell me if you have received that sixty-dollar money order or not. I thought you would save that for my furlough, if you got it.

Honey, I sure hope nothing happens to stop my furlough. Let me know if you would like to meet up with me at my folks. Is this okay by you or would you have me come there for a couple of days and then go on up to my home together? Don't make me no difference. The only thing is if we have the money to do it that way. Whatever you think is best and what you want to do is fine with me. Let me know which way you want to do it so we can come to an agreement.

I started this letter yesterday and will finish it today. Boy, am I down in the dumps. Other boys are going on their furloughs and I am not yet. I sure am anxious to get mine.

I've got to get my washing done today. Haha. I sure would make a good washerwoman. I'll bet I could be a good housekeeper too. I would probably make you more dirt than three people could clean up.

There ain't much I can write about, only how much I love you more than anything in this world. You can tell the world that your husband really loves you when he can't be there with you. If I could hold you in my arms, I would be more happier than I am out here.

About going to the show, Honey. They are shown here on the base so I don't have to leave camp to see one. About that dancing. Well, if you can't learn me maybe after the war is over we can learn together then if you want to. I sure wish it would be soon as I am getting lonesome for you.

If I remember right, we got married on September 10th or 11th. It has been about six months since I've seen you. That is a long time for me. You know, I've been in the army for two years and two months today. That sure is a long time, too. I just hope I won't have to serve that long again.

Well, darling, it is time for me to say aloha and go to bed. It has been nice talking to you. Talk back to me soon. Okay? I will always love you.

Your husband, Charles

(Author's note: They were married November 9, 1942

Well, I had better close and do my washing. Honey, tell the children I said hello and give them my love and I will be seeing them before very long. Tell my wife that I love her very dearly or does she know it by now?

I love you. Honest I do.

Your husband, Charles

To The Swellest Wife a Fellow Could Ever Have,
Hello Darling,

I am very lonesome right now. I wrote a letter earlier but feel like writing another. My thoughts are all of you tonight. I have reason to be lonesome then since you can't be here with me.

But Darling, I have thought many times of what your mother said that it would be harder if we didn't wait until after the war to get married. Now I know she was right. But, I thank God we were together for the little while we were. That is something I can never be sorry about. Honey, may God bring us together soon. That would surely make me happy.

I sure am lonely for you tonight. Do you think we will be happy together, now? I do. And you would get one of the best squeezes one ever got. I would love you all night if I were there. Honey, you told me you liked to be loved. I would love you like anything when we are together again. I write awhile, then, I stop and think of you awhile. And then I wonder why it takes so long for me to write a letter. The stars are flickering just like the way they were the night we saw them together.

Well, Honey, I will close for now and go to bed. It is about that time. I will say a prayer for you when I get in bed and hope to have nice dreams of you also.

So, bye for now. Give the children my love. Don't forget I love you.

I LOVE YOU SWAK

We are suppose to move from here to Santa Rosa, California. I will let you know when we do move and send you the address.

1943

To the One Dearest to me, My Wife, Cora Mae WARD,

I am proud of that name . . . are you? Well, I will try to write a line or so. Christmas is getting close. My Mom sent a box of cookies the other day. She can't be too mad at me.

I went to the doctor the other day to see why my mouth was sore. He said I had trench mouth. Now isn't that something? My heart did about three quick beats too many when he told me that. He said it wouldn't take very long to cure if I did what he told me to. I sure will. I must have gotten it from drinking out of someone elses's cup.

I guess we are going to have to leave here between now and Christmas. We are going to Salem Oregon. That is all I know for now. Will tell you the rest when I find out.

Hey, I hope it had quit raining when you all butchered. It bet it was all wet while butchering in the rain. It would be like trying to dry clothes in the rain. Honey, I sure would like to have been there to help you butcher but I probably would have been in the way. My pop always said I worked harder to get out of work than I did working. But maybe he was kidding.

Honey, if I were ever afraid of marrying you, it was myself I was afraid of. I wanted to marry you the first time I saw you. I was afraid I would not be man enough to support and treat you as I should. I know now I just want the chance to do all I can for you and the children. I know there is one way to show you I love you when I get out of here. You see all I am trying to say to you is that nothing I can do will ever repay for what you have brought into my life. You have shown me that there is such a thing as true love. You have learned me to trust in that love. I never believed or trusted anyone or anybody until I met you. So you see Honey, I have put all my love and trust in you and I pray and trust in God that He will keep it that way. I have never written a letter like this before, so I ask you to believe what I've said in it. I ain't never meant anything more in my whole life. So keep hoping, be good and it will be okay in the end.

Honey, how is everything going on there? Everything here is always the same. Honey, you will never know just how hard it was to leave you but we all got a job to do here. We don't like it but we have to do it. When we finally get together, we have a job to do together. It will be a long one but one I look forward with all my heart to doing. If you and I pull together we can make it a job that will last all our lives. One you won't get tired of. My sis says there isn't anything better than married life if it is a happy one. I want ours to be happy all our lives. I just want to get there so we can begin.

How is everything back there? Everything here is always the same. I sure get disgusted just waiting around. Do you? I can't wait to get back to you so I can keep you happy. Do you think I can? I know you can me.

Are you getting any answers from my folks? My dad says he is glad I married you and not some one else. He really thinks I've done right. Mother will too, when she sees you. I hope that won't be too long.

When you get this letter, I hope you are all okay and happy. As for me, outside of being lonely, I am okay. How are the children now? Does Betty remember me? I'll bet she does. How is Jr.? He sure is some guy.

Well, Darling, once again so long. Be good and write soon. I love you more than anything in this world.

Your husband, Charles W. Ward I love you I love you I love you SWAK

Dearest Cora Mae,

Well, Honey I just got back from the main garrison to get those pillow cases. I didn't get the kind I wanted to get for you and your mother. These are all I could get and the ones I am sending you. I will keep trying and as soon as I can get the ones I want, I will get those for you. The war is making it hard getting some things. I haven't had a letter from you in two days now. I haven't said anything to hurt you have I?

You said Bill had to go to Georgia for his exam. You know he probably would have come out here as some of the new boys who said they were from Tennessee and Georgia so I was hoping he would be sent here also. We leave her Monday, so start sending my mail to my new address. I wish I could be in Tennessee now. Boy, would we do some cutting up or would we?

Honey, has your ex been bothering you? I hope not. Have you been getting my letters? I haven't missed a day writing you for quite a spell. Please let me know how things are going by you. Are you getting along alright? How are the children getting along? I am being as good as I can.

You know, I never will forget Betty. She is a little spitfire, isn't she? Is Jr. going to school regularly? He probably doesn't like it any better than I did. But he will never regret going, in the end. Does Louise remember me? Tell the boys to write me a line in some of your letters. I would like to hear from them.

Well, Darling I must close. It is time for lights out and ours is the only one on. The guard will be jumping on us, if we don't. How are your father and mother feeling these days? I'll bet she didn't think I was going to send that pillow case, did she? But I was always slow in doing things, even in marrying you. Haha. You will never know how I feel being away from you. It seems like a year since I was there. I will make you wish I wasn't so in love with you. I will be loving you night and day. You will probably run me off, won't you? Would you?

Well, Honey tell your folks hello for me.

Goodbye for now,

Your husband, Charles SWAK (a picture of two hearts with an arrow drawn through it).

1943

To My Dearest Wife, Cora Mae,

Well, I am late writing to you again, but we have been so busy moving to another camp. I haven't even had time to mail the ones I have already written. I will mail them with this one.

I am in the east garrison at Fort Ord now so you can send my mail there. Honey I sure am a lonesome boy now. We just got into this camp a couple of hours ago and we are pretty well settled for the night. We had a real cold trip up here. We traveled in open scout cars and trucks and it was pretty cold. I sure am glad to get out of the desert.

I wish I could be with you., as I need a good girl to hug and kiss. Haha. I mean it though. Maybe a miracle will happen and we can be together before too long. You think I am probably being silly, but being away from you is enough to make any boy silly.

We've got hot water to take a bath and wash here. That is one good thing. My thumb is just about well. A little stiff, but that is all.

I can't think of much more to say. I love you. Tell everyone I said hello and good luck. Tell the children hello and give them my love.

So answer soon. I will write more tomorrow night.

Your devoted husband, Charles

P.S. Honey, I've got to write more as I am not contented unless I do. You were saying in your last letter that you had been hurt so much that it doesn't take much to hurt you and kill your love for anyone.

If I ever say anything in my letters to hurt you, don't get mad at me. So, if I do and don't know it, what can I do? Let me know because I need and want you to love and believe in me, no matter what happens. So until we can be together again as I know we will be, we must continue to love one another.

You see I have my whole heart wrapped up in you and I won't do anything to hurt you when we are living our lives together. You might think I talk funny but see I have been around and have had lots of experiences. So I know you are the girl I was looking for. I like a kind hearted person and you are the only one who showed me your own true self without trying to make me think you were this or that. You were the same girl I met on the bus at Nashville when I came back to see you and that counts for always. Be yourself, Honey, don't ever let me lose faith in you. You will always be the same Cora Mae as you were when I first met you, won't you?

So, until we meet again, never again to part, I'll say I'll always be true to you. Charles

1943

To the One I Love More Than Anything in the World, My Cora Mae.

Just a line to say howdy. Everything is okay except for my finger. I liked to cut it off this morning. I stuck it in a can of green beans and got my finger instead. If it hadn't been for the bone in my finger, it would have gone all the way through. I'll have a nice scar but I still am a lucky stiff.

Say, I haven't heard from you for a week. It is probably slow getting sent here from school. I am still working in the kitchen but I am getting disgusted. I don't know if I will ever get my rating back again or not. They are probably afraid I will get into an argument with the captain again if they did. I guess they want to make sure I am able to take orders like I should. That is my problem I think. I don't like to take orders from anyone. I don't know how it will be to take orders from my wife. I think I will like to take orders from her.

There is some blood from my finger on this page. I hope you can read this. My hands are shaking like a leaf. Maybe I am about to have a nervous breakdown. Haha

Honey, how are you getting along? Did you receive the step-ins I sent?

How are our children coming along? Okay I hope. I sure hope I can get a furlough soon so I can come to see you folks, especially my wife. We are going to see my folks somehow when I get my furlough. Honey, you ought to see this country out here. It sure is pretty. Honey, does your brother still do a lot of loving with his wife? Boy, I got a lot of loving to make up. Think I could ever make it up? You can bet I will always try to make you happy. Haha

Honey, I can't think of much more to say except I love you more than you will ever know. Always remember, I love you and that is the truth if I ever have told the truth.

Your husband, Charles SWAK

P.S. You are going to have to overlook my writing as I am writing this with my thumb all wrapped with a bandage.

I guess we are going to be moved out now. I will send you my address As soon as I have it. We will probably go to the coast for a coast guard outfit or an anti aircraft training. Don't worry about me. If I should never get back to you, I can honestly say I have spent the finest week I know with the girl the Lord made for me.

How is everyone there? Take good care of the children for me. Tell Jr. to be a good fellow for me until I get back.

Well I will wait until the pictures are in and send them along. I hope these are better than the last batch.

To The One I Love, Cora Mae,

Well, just a few lines to finish this letter I started last night, but didn't mail yet. We leave tomorrow, so I won't be able to write again until day after tomorrow. We got all our gear packed and other things ready for an early start. Honey, I hope this gets to you real soon so you can start sending my mail to Santa Rosa.

We will be on patrol when we get there all the time. It will probably be cold writing as it will be at night when it is cold and we will be on duty twenty four hours a day. I got one air-mail stamp, so I will send it to you and you can use it to mail your letter to me.

Send my mail to Santa Rosa. I hope this finds you as well as I am. Tell the children hello for me. So, bye for now. You will always be with me.

Your husband, Charles SWAK

1943

To The Best Girl I Ever Knew, MY Wife, Cora Mae,

Well, another day has gone by and no letter from you. I suppose you are busy and writing every day can get old. But for me since I have been in the troops, I have lots of time to write. I missed two or three days when we are moving as we are all busy then. We have been going on five-mile hikes every couple of days. I wish we would take them every day. It makes time go faster.

I can't think of much to say, only I wish I was in Tennessee. Don't you? Or do you? Tell your sis I said hello and watch out when she goes to the mailbox and who she goes with. Tell everyone else hello for me also.

I love you, I love you, I love you. Is there anything else you want me to write in my letters to prove I love you? I wish I could chew your ears for you, just for devilment.

Well, Honey, good luck and best wishes for now.

Your loving husband, Charles

Dearest Darling Cora Mae,

Just a few lines to say hello and ask how all are getting along? Fine I hope. I am okay but I do get very impatient with this war. I get to thinking of what kind of job I could do when we start our lives together. It can't come too soon for me. Don't you think so?

Tell Jesse and Robert I said he should watch out for those girls as they are bad medicine. They will get into their hair and pull it out. Haha. I didn't get no letter today. I sure miss it but you probably have just as hard a time finding something to talk about much as I do.

How are the children coming along? Fine I hope. I do a lot of thinking about you and what we best do when I get back. I can't seem to see anything better than for us to stay on a farm or work toward getting one of out own to run. It would take a lot of hard work and heartache. But I think you and I loving each other like we do it would work out. I want you to ask your daddy what he thinks best. You know we were both raised on a farm and I think it is in our blood. I want his advice because I want our life starting out on the right track. If we can possibly have it that way. Your dad can probably give us some good advice as he is older and knows more about how things work than we do. My dad says "once a farmer always a farmer." Do you think that's true? I would like to know what you think we should do. You know you have never said what we should do. You know, Honey, from now on it is fifty-fifty. So give me some idea what you think you want to do.

Well, I got to sign off now. Tell Mom & Pop I said hello. I call my folks Pop & Mom, so I guess I can call yours that too. Tell Bill I wish he could get to come out here if he has to go. I hope he doesn't for your folks' sake. Tell him I said make my wife be good and I will do the same for him, someday. How is Roy getting along?

For now I'll say so long. Write and tell how you are getting along. Tell your sis to watch out for that curly headed guy or she will be doing the same thing we did when we went to the mailbox. Tell her to watch out who she goes to the mailbox with. All kidding aside, I am glad we went to the mailbox with you. Are you?

Love & Best Wishes,

Your husband, Charles Wesley Ward.

SWAK

To The One I Love & Adore, My Wife Cora Mae,

Dearest Cora Mae,

I love you. Well, here it is another day and all is well. It leaves me okay but not happy. I didn't get any letter from you today and missed it very much. I got the last two letters you sent and kissed each one of your kisses that you put there. Sure wish it could have been your lips instead of just paper. I just rolled a cigarette and wish you could be here to smoke it with me.

Honey, we got places to get pictures made but the cheapest will be five dollars. And that is clear out of reason for me. I will wait until I can get it for less. You don't think my pictures are worth that much do you?

Honey, tell Robert to send me a line every once in awhile. How is Roy and his wife getting along? Does she ever say anything about how we were sitting in that chair? Haha. I bet she did. I can imagine how you women talk when you are alone. Just like men do when they are alone. Do you know any stories? You know men don't hear many stories when they are in the army. Oh no . . . not many. Haha

Have you got any more letters from my folks or my sister or brother? I sure wish I could be with you. I sure am getting tired of army life. I pray for the day when this will be over. That sure will be a happy day for me.

It has been two years since I have been in here and sure have learned a lot. One thing I learned is who I love and want to be with the rest of my life. I wish I could be there pretty quick so we can get started on what we want to do with the rest of our lives.

Honey, do you think I will be too much of a bother for you. I hope not. I'll try not to be. I can't think of much to say except how much I love you and would like to be holding you in my arms. You don't know how I wish that. I would squeeze you until you turned blue. I would like to make a pass at you. Could I? Tell Bill I sure wish I could be there to see them. I bet Bill is easy to kid, isn't he?

Well, tell the children I said hello. From one who is lonesome for you. I love you, truly I do.

Your husband, Charles SWAK I Love You

1943

To Cora Mae, The Only One I Will Ever Love,

Dearest Darling,

Well, it is about time for me to write. I have been very lax about writing, but we have really been busy all this week. I have been about half sick. It seems every time I eat I get cramps in my belly. But it is better today. I hope it stays that way.

Well, I completed my first month of school today. We had a test on it and I got one hundred ninety five out of two hundred. Not bad, huh?

I haven't heard from anyone for about a week now. I suppose you are like me. You can't write if you don't have anything to write about. But, Darling, don't go too long without writing, as I miss the letters very much.

I haven't heard about the allotment have you? They ought to be sending a notice to one of us pretty soon, I would think. But things like that takes a lot of time. I guess I am just too impatient.

I think I will go to a show tonight, just to break the monotony. I don't go very often but it is the only past time they have around here. They have dances about once a week. But I can't dance so I don't go. I will have you teach me so we can go out when I get home. Would you teach me to dance?

I suppose I had better cut this short. We got some new boys that are going to be cooks. So I will be glad to get back to my old outfit as everyone here is a stranger and I don't like to be around strangers too long. Boy, do I know who I would like to be around. Can you guess?

Have you heard from my folks lately? I'd write to them and give them heck for not corresponding with you, but Honey, they are probably busy and can't write much. I sure do hope I get a letter tonight. We only get our mail once a day out here.

Well I did receive your letter today telling me you have had influenza. I hope you are better by the time you get this. I also got your mom's letter.

Honey, about that writing on the back of those pictures. You know I would only be too glad to marry her again and I would like to sleep with her again, because I love her more than any thing else in this world. And about that furlough . . . I can't say, as we never know what is going on. If we stay up on the coast any longer, we should be getting one. I don't know until they say. I hope soon.

I also hope this war ends soon. Everyday I spend here is just one less day from our happiness. And Honey, I am counting those days until I get back with you.

I am glad that you and Bill like those pillowslips that I sent. I hope Polly likes hers too. Honey, I meant every word written on your slip. I truly love you with all my heart. I am glad you are still wearing my ring. I hope you will wear it the rest of our lives and I will always try to make you proud to wear it.

I can't think of much more to say. I will write more later. I will try to do better next week. Please remember you mean all the world to me and always will.

Love, Charles W. Ward SWAK

1943

To My Wife, Cora Mae,

I am in bed writing this. That just shows what a lazy husband you have. I haven't had a letter from you in three days. You aren't going to let me down are you? Did I say something that hurt you? Don't forget we promised to do our arguing in a quiet way and try to see each other's point of view. So if I said or did anything you didn't like or you thought was wrong, let me know so I can remedy the situation.

Everything here is okay except for me. How are the children getting along? Okay I hope.

Have you heard from any of my kinfolk yet? If so, what did they say? I am anxious to know. Honey, I wish we could start our lives together soon. Every year that passes now is one year less with you. Our life together is getting shorter.

Honey, about that allotment. I can't let you know about it until I find out. The only way I am going to find out is when they take it out of my paycheck. If that does not happen this month, I am going to find out what's wrong. You see, it means just as much to me as it does to you. Because the longer it takes means that it is just that much longer it ain't getting to you as I figured on. I will try to explain what I mean. The government pays me fifty dollars a week. When the allotment is okayed, the government will take twenty five dollars out of my fifty and add twenty-eight dollars to it and send that to you. So you see when the allotment goes through that would mean that just twenty-two dollars I am losing. So you see the sooner it goes through, the better it will be for both of us. I hope it goes through soon.

Well, I had better close. It is time for lights out. Write as often as you can as your letters are all I have to look forward to. You are all I have for happiness now. So please don't forget me.

So Honey, now I say so long. Tell everyone I said hello. Keep your chin up.

Yours, forever, your husband Charles SWAK

1943

Just a line to let you know I am still alive. OK? I guess I don't get much writing time. I got sent back to my old outfit. I guess they didn't want me to go to mess sergeant school. My captain, I mean. The captain and I are on opposite sides of the fence. So I can see why I wasn't allowed to go to school. But I don't care. Every dog has its' day.

About that good news . . . my outfit are getting furloughs again, so I should be getting one in about three or four months, if nothing happens. I guess I won't be getting paid for a few months so my money for a furlough will be pretty short. When I got back, about half my equipment was gone. I don't know whether I will have to pay for it or not. I hope not.

Honey, I hope this finds you okay. If not, let me know.

From one who loves you the most.

Your husband, Charles

I love you. SWAK I will write more next time.

To The sweetest Girl On Earth, To My One & Only Forever,

Dearest Cora Mae, I love you

Well, Darling, I got your letter of the 25th. I am glad the allotment is coming through now. They haven't been taking any out of my pay yet. I don't quite understand it. They will probably take it out all at once. I hope it doesn't get all tangled up. But I am glad you are receiving the money. I will still send all I can. You can save it for me or use it. I want you to let me know when you get the money from me so if things go wrong, I can try to get it worked out. Also, I want to know if you are receiving it. We get paid tomorrow and if I get the full amount, I'll know they still are not taking it out. I don't think it will affect your allotment though. Now Honey, use the check as you like, just do right. Okay?

I sure hope you have good luck with the kids. Did you vaccinate them? Or do you folks vaccinate your kids. My folks always vaccinate theirs'. It keeps them from getting the cholera. Be careful and not let any of them get my dinner, won't you? Haha.

I've asked you in previous letters before, but you have yet to answer. What do your folks think of me? I don't ask that to be nosy . . . I only want to understand them. You see, Honey, I will always be looking out for our own good. And I would like for your folks to see it that way. Do they think I am doing right by you?

You can tell your brothers for me they are lucky not to have to go into the army. I sure envy them. But we've got to understand some of us have to be in here. I don't know for sure what Bill and Polly's good news is but I can read between the lines. It wouldn't be one of those things, would it? A baby?

No, I don't know about the story of the man who rode the train for the first time, but, Honey I am all ears. But I could tell you for sure I would be in the bunk first. I don't know when I can come home. I hope soon.

Well, Honey, I can't think of much more to say so I'll say so long. Say hello to everyone for me. Give our children my love. Honey I wish I were there for many reasons than one. I am going to bed and try hard to dream about you. I hope I do dream of you.

I'll close saying I love you dearly.

Your husband, Charles SWAK SWAK SWAK.

To My Dearest Cora Mae,

Well, Honey, here I am again. So often when I write, I run out of things to say. So let's change the subject now and write about our selves. I will write you my life history and you will write me yours.

I was born and raised in Payne, Ohio. We lived there eighteen years and then moved to Grover Hill. I was a bad guy in general, giving my folks trouble mostly. I played hooky from school until they threatened to kick me out. I got average grades and lots of whippings quite often in my freshman year. I worked as a carpenter one year, then as a painter for about a year. I worked in the sugar beet fields a lot.

I went into the C.C.C. for about another year and then started farming. I also got mixed up with some women in between. Nothing very serious. Was in the boy scouts for awhile. I also drove truck. Mom said I was the best boy of the family, but I have to wonder about that.

When I come home, I was thinking of taking up farming. Would you like that? Do you like to farm.

I can't think of much more to say now. I haven't gotten a letter from you in a long time. Honey, don't wait until I write you. They keep us very busy here. I like your letters so write as much and often as you can.

Have they got a bunch of new recruits at Ft. Forrest? The place was almost deserted when I left there for San Diego. Well, Honey, it is dinnertime so I've got to go.

I hope this leaves you as it leaves me. And you know what that is. Please don't forget me as I will be back in a year. Just kidding. Just joking. War is breaking out now but we will meet again somewhere, someday.

Yours Forever, Closing with all my love, C.W. Ward

P.S.

You said you wish you were out here with me. I do too, but I told your mother I would not take you away. The children needs you there and the expense of you living out here will be too much for us.

Maybe this damn war will be over soon and we won't have to be apart. You don't realize what it would mean to me to be with you forever, but we will have to wait until this war is over.

Honey, I've got to close for now. Loving you forever

Your husband, C.W. Ward.

My Dearest Wife, I love you,

Dear Cora Mae,

Well, Darling, I received your letters today. I sure was glad to get them. It is funny you got my letters all at the same time. Honey, about that cake. It would hardly spoil in that short of time. It may have gotten smashed in the mail or someone else got to it and ate it.

Who sent you the earrings? Was there a name on it?

I just heard a dirty joke from one of the boys. I thought about telling it to you. But I better not, I guess. It is corny anyway. I sure wish I were there to kiss your lips and smoke your cigarettes. I did that the last time when I was there, didn't I? I felt so close to you then. I have thought of many things we did when I was there the last time.

If you wash and iron for your mother as well as your own self, you've got a job. I'm glad of the way you talk in your letters now. I am glad you love and trust in me. That is what I want you to do.

Now, to give you heck about that money. I didn't want to offend you or to seem nosey, but if you have saved forty-three dollars, why that is more than I can see how you could have saved that much. That is yours and I want you to use it if you need it. I only want you to save enough so that if I get a furlough, we will have enough for me to get there. But I don't want you to worry because if you have saved forty three dollars, You certainly don't have anything to be ashamed of. You sure have done better than I could have. You are going to be the cashier of our household. Well, I can't think of much more to say. So, I must close for now. So until we meet again, I'll say so long for now.

Your husband, Charles

SWAK

I just got your letter, so I will answer it now and send it with this one. Honey, I know my folks will know that you will be a good wife for me, even if they never see you. My folks believe what I say and trust me to know my own mind. They know that I would not have married anyone who would not be a good wife to me. So for that reason, they will know that you are all that I say you are.

As for you stepping out on me, I never wrote anything in my letter to make you think I thought you would. And I didn't mean it that way. I have trust in you and that is the reason I never thought of it. I never had and I want you to do the same. Well, Darling, if none of us does the other wrong, it will come out in the end.

I am sending the rest of your letter back. I want you to explain how you mean it. The writing on back of the seal, I mean. I guess I won't kiss anyone if you both are going to get on me. Haha. But if you say you don't like it then I won't as I don't want you mad at me and would not do anything to spoil our love.

Tell the children I send my love and kisses to them. Honey, remember I will always love and be true to you the rest of my life.

Honey, I hope you can read this letter and make it out. What does the word (can't read) mean that I've underlined on the envelope? I work at night and sleep during the day time.

Adios,
C.W.Ward

To the Sweetest & Dearest Wife, Cora Mae,

Cora Mae, I love you, I love you.

Well another day has gone by and all is well. I answered a letter to my folks and thought I would drop you a lone too.

Well, Honey, we made sandwiches for seventy-five people and it turned out they were all officers and they didn't like the way we put the peanut butter on them. We didn't spread the peanut butter thin enough to suit them. And some of the bread we used was too dry. Boy, did we get told off. I am going to have to be more careful who I make sandwiches for. * I wish you were here. Maybe you could learn me to make them right. Do you suppose?

You probably think my being a cook is funny but this is how I look at it. If I can cook and bake a little and if things go wrong for us on the farm or anything, if I need to I will have something to fall back on so we could get by. I figure it might help us later on. Do you think so? They say a cook can always get a job. That is why I took this job.

Honey, I hope when you get this you are happy and okay. It leaves me well but not very happy. You know the word happy has a very big meaning. Don't you think it has?

---

* Dad lost his rating over the peanut caper.

Well, Darling, I've got to close at this time. Always remember I love you, truly I do. With all my heart and soul. Give the children my love. So I say, so long for now and with all my love,

Your husband, Charles XOXOXO

To The One I Love Best, Cora Mae.

Well, Honey, I will try to write a few lines, but what, I don't know. The weather is raining and cool. The sun doesn't want to shine for some reason. How is it there?

How would you like a big kiss and hug about right now? I would like it very much. Say, Honey would you still love me when my carburetor don't carburete any more or my generator don't generate any more? Think you will love me when I get old and full of pain and there is no smile on my windowpane? Do you? Huh? Don't mind if I get that way every now and then. There is no fool like an old fool. You say you love me. Oh you don't? Oh you do. Don't you? You do, don't you? Now do you? I love you like any thing.

Two frogs frigging sitting on a float croaking. Two dogs sitting on a bank, barking. Can you make it out? You know what is meant by frigging, don't you? So be careful with that word and who sees this letter or who you say it to.

Say, Honey, can you tell me how long it would take a cross-eyed grasshopper to kick the suds out of a dill pickle? A fellow told me one time that when a fellow gets married and his friend has none, I will see to it that my wife will get him some. Do you know what the diaper said to the baby? I will cover the waterfront. Honey, do you see the point? If you do, don't sit on it, Do you know the difference between an elephant and a bag of peanuts? Let me know if you do in your next letter.

Well, Darling, enough of that kind of stuff. I know some more but they are pretty vulgar. If you want to hear them, let me know.

How are Bill and Jesse doing with their wives? Boy, I wish I were there with mine. I would be so very happy. But sometime we will be together and we will show them, won't we? Or will we? We sure can try anyway. You say you were looking to be with me soon. I hope you are right. I hope to get a furlough soon or pray this war ends sooner.

I haven't heard anything of your sister, Martha. I she still around? I never will forget how she grins and smiles like a bashful girl. She isn't any more bashful than I was. Has she got a boyfriend? Tell her to watch out or she will be embarking on the sea of matrimony.

I wish I was holding you in my arms right now. I would be so happy. I pray every night I will be with you in the near future. And boy, I hope my prayers are answered. If I had you here, I would squeeze you until you hollered Indian!

I sure would like one of those long kisses like we had together. I would give my leg for one. When I get to thinking of you being my wife, I get a happy feeling in my heart. I know my love for you is the truest love there is, cause the way I feel is enough to tell me that. I will never find anyone to equal you in my heart or anyone to take your place.

I must close for now. So until I write again, I'll say goodbye and good luck. Say hello to our children for me.

From your husband who is mighty proud to be your husband. Honest I do. I love you my darling.

Your husband, Charles SWAK

Casper, California

To The One I Love, Cora Mae,

I received your letter and was glad to get it. I am glad you are okay. I am okay but in low spirits. I guess that is getting to be natural with me. I guess I am just too anxious to see you or something. Boy, I sure hope all you'll ever hear is the plant bed steamer's whistle and never have to hear a an air raid siren. I bet you got a kick out of it when the whistle scared the children, but I bet they didn't.

About me not sending you any money, Honey. When I get more money than I need I will send some to you. Because, if I do, then I won't spend it. You can save the money for me. If I get a furlough, I'll write you for it. It will cost me about sixty five dollars to get home on. If we try, I think we can save that much, don't you? They are liable not to pay me for two months when they find the mistake on the allotment check. They were suppose to take twenty two dollars out of my check each time you get an allotment check. They haven't yet but when they find out they will hold up my pay for two months until it is righted again. But I don't care as long as you get your check.

I got a letter from my folks. They are going to raise twenty acres of popcorn this year. They also got another tractor. I think they will have more machinery than they need pretty soon. Dad is selling his team of horses. I wish he would keep them and work horses more than tractors. I think there is more profit in working horses than letting them stand idle. But Dad has his mind made up and who am I to say anything.

I'll be glad when we are in the farming business by ourselves, won't you? You know, I have a vision of you and I having our own farming equipment to run it. We could live a free and happy live with no obligations to no one. I think that is the best way to have things. We can't have it that way at first but that is what I would be willing to work toward, if you will stick with me on those ideas.

To have a home of our own and own our own things. So no one can tell us to move or how to do things. Don't you think that is the best way to live?

Honey, I started this letter three days ago but I got sent back to my old outfit so I will send you my address. I don't have much to write but I may have some good news in a little while.

I'll say I love you. Will write more when I can.

Your husband, Charles SWAK

P.S. Well, Honey, before I mail this, I will write a few more lines. I got your letter with my Pop's letter in it. I am glad he wrote you. I knew he would take our marriage in good spirits. When we show him how much we love each other, he will be glad we are together. I can imagine how you felt when you were at your folks and all were there with their loved ones. I ask God not to keep us apart another Christmas. I am glad for Bill and Robert who are able to stay home where they are needed.

Well, Darling, can't think of much else to write so will close. Remember I will always love you. Don't ever doubt me.

From your husband, Charles

P.S. Be good and I will do the same. I love you SWAK

December 25, 1943
California

My Wife, Cora Mae,

Well, Darling, Christmas will be over in about four hours. I just got back from seeing a picture show. It was "My Gal Sal". It was a good show. I wish you could have been here to see it with me. It would have been lots brighter.

I have spent my day doing nothing except thinking of you. Honey, I don't know what I would do if I didn't have you to think of. The only pleasure I have now is thinking and dreaming of you. I get to thinking of you and I get a happy feeling in my heart and things seem more pleasant. So you see, I really got more of a right to say I love you as you are my wife and I am so proud of her.

If you ever leave me I would die if you should ever lose your love for me. You are all I got to look forward to. You are the light of my world and happiness. I only want to live for you. You see, we are only a nation apart, but my love for you makes me feel much closer to you.

Well, I had better sign off for now. I love you with all my heart and God willing, we will be together sooner than we might think. Tell your folks I said hello and thank them for my wife.

MERRY CHRISTMAS MY DARLING.

Your loving husband, Charles. SWAK XOXOX

Here is another insurance policy. Keep it in a safe place as it could be important. So don't lose it. I also got a letter from Mom Silverfoot. I will enclose it with this letter.

Love & Kisses

Charles

1943

To The Sweetest Wife I Know, my Cora Mae,

Well, Honey just a few lines to let you know I am okay and hope you are the same. We are getting a little less rain the last day or so or I am just getting use to it. When you receive this I hope your flu is over and forgot about.

I got a letter from my brother the other day, the one who wrote you. He said he had rented a farm for himself. I have seen it and it is really a good place. I hope he does good with it. I told him he needed a nice wife like mine to keep him straightened out on his weak points. Aren't I right? Do you think you can keep me straightened out? Make me be good? Boy, you have your job cut out for you if you do. Haha.

I got a letter from my folks. They said they were all okay. I guess we get paid Saturday or Monday. Then I can send you some money as I figured on. I was made PFC, which means Private First Class. That means four more dollars per month for us. I am going back up slowly. If I ever get my sergeant rating back, I will try to hang on as long as I am in the army. Then I can send you more money. But if I do get it back, I will be lucky. I was foolish to give it up in the first place. If I had known I was going to get married, I wouldn't have done it. But then it didn't make no difference then.

When they send me to cooks and bakers school, I am going to try to get stationed in one of the army's bakery. Then I might do better. I hope I can make it.

Honey, are you all still stripping tobacco? Think I could? I sure would like to, wouldn't you? We had a movie out here the other day. It was a good show. Wish you could have been here to see it with me.

We are getting about seventy-five new men this week. They sent thirty men up into the mountains to look for an airplane that went down up there somewhere. We haven't heard back from them so I guess they haven't located it yet. I heard it had just come back from someplace where the war is in progress. I just heard mail call. I hope I get a letter.

I didn't get one. Honey I get down in the dumps when I don't get a letter from you. I look for them every mail call. I know it is hard to think of new things to say but just writing the same old things is okay by me. I know you are there and thinking of me. That is what being married is all about.

How are Bill and Polly doing? Are they being good like we were? Do you think? I got the fun of coming back to you. That will be like starting all over again. We sure will be happy when that day comes, won't we? I dream of getting out of here and you and I and the children having a home of our own. Just living and loving you and them. Sometimes I almost cry when I think of it. Someday we are going to have things our way, no matter what we have to go through. We will have a place of our own so no one can say, "Well you have to move". I don't like things that way. I want to do things as we see fit. You see I want to do it so we will always be happy as we want. To be happy, we have to live free of obligations that can keep people from being happy. Those are what I want you to be free of.

I will try to write your Mom & Pop. I haven't written them for a spell. Keep on sending my letters to this address. How are the children getting along? Do they remember me? I can never forget them. Does your ex come to see them anymore? Does your old admirer bother you very much? Wish I were there. You would probably get tired of me bothering you. Hah! But, Darling I do wish I were there if only to bother you. I would try to do a good job of that.

I don't see how your folks can put their faith in me. I have never done anything for them except to bother them for one week. I will try to live up to their faith in me, though. But I can surely take good care of their daughter when I get the chance. I use to be pretty good at farming when I was home. I hope I can do it again after the war. I hope so for our sakes. You don't know how I dream of getting out of here.

Well, I had better close so I can write to Mom & Dad to say hello. Tell your sis to be careful who she walks to the mailbox with. Honey, I will never forget that walk we took to the mailbox. Would you go to the mailbox and let me talk you into getting married again? I want you to answer this question in my next letter. I wish I was there just to go to the mailbox to see for yourself.

Well I will close with you always on my mind.

Your husband, Charles, SWAK

1943

Dearest Cora Mae,

I received your letter of the 23rd and 25th. Both of them came together. One of them must have gotten an earlier reservation on a train.

Honey, I am okay and hope you are okay and not mad in any way. Don't you ever think I am sorry of our marriage. If you ever ask me a silly question like that again, I will give you a good whipping when I come back. Honey, I will never be sorry I married you. If I ever did get sorry of it, I will tell you. But don't think of that happening because it won't. So I ask you please don't think of that in any way I would be sorry of marrying you. I don't want you to think of that. You've made me happy and I am trusting in you to always make me happy. I love you so much I could never be sorry of marrying you. I love you with all my heart and soul.

You tell your daddy I sure appreciate what he is doing for me and when I get out of here, I promise to take good care of you for the rest of my life. I will try to repay him for what he is doing for me.

Well, Honey, they just found the plane I told you had been missing.

I guess all the people were dead. It had just flown back from Hawaii and couldn't find a place to land.

I am going back to cooking school tomorrow. I sent in town today money order for thirty four dollars. I will send it in this letter, so let me know when you get it. You can get it cashed when you go to town.

Honey, you don't need to worry about me stopping loving you. The only thing that would make me mad would be if you stopped writing to me. I want you to answer these questions in your next letter. Tell me the real truth about it and don't worry of hurting my feelings. I want to know how you feel about it and I want the truth. You know we promised to never lie to each other. What I want to know is do you think I am doing right by you. ? Do you think I am sending you the right amount of my pay? Do I send you enough or do you think not? Do you believe me when tell you I love you? Do you think I am doing right by you? And if I ain't, tell me how you want me to do. Tell me your honest opinion about these things. Because, if I ain't doing right by you, then I can correct myself.

You see, what I want is your love and I want you to know I am willing to do right as right can be to get your love from you. Honey, there isn't anything I want worse than your honest love and I am willing to do anything I can so you will be happy to give it to me. You see I am your husband and fate has given us a hard path and it really hurts to be kept away from you. When I get to thinking of you and how much you mean to me, I almost cry. Sometimes I think I ain't doing right by you but there isn't anything I can do if you don't write to tell me what I should do. So when you answer this, tell me your honest opinion. I don't want you to think by this letter that I don't love you because I do. More than anything in this world. All I live for is to come back to you because I know that is the only place I will be happy. I hope God will let me live so I can come back to you and prove my love is as true and honest as any love can be.

So, Honey, I must close at this time. Tell all the folks I said hello. Give my love to our children. From one who will always love you no matter what anyone says or do or what happens. So don't think you have done anything wrong and always believe me when I say I love you and am very proud to have you as my wife. What other people say or do don't mean anything to me as you are everything to me. As long as I have you, I will be very satisfied and happy with you. Do you understand? All I want to do is to make you see is that I do love you and want you to love me.

So now, I will say so long,

Your husband, Charles, SWAK

To The Sweetest Girl I Know, Cora Mae,

Well, Honey, I will start this now . . . Don't know if I can get it finished as I slipped off from the kitchen to write it. I sent you a letter this morning but I was trying to tell you how much I love you and how dear you are to me. To be near and with you is all the happiness I will ever ask for anymore.

I only got three weeks of school left. I will be glad when that is over with, I think. Have you heard from my folks lately? They ain't wrote me for over a week now. They ain't much for writing. They are like me. They like to get letters but are too lazy to answer them. Haha. Remember, I told you, you had a lazy husband. Haha. Just kidding. One day you will know whether I am lazy or no good.

I am sure anxious for that day to come. Honey, we will talk things over when we are together. I believe we will be able to talk it over then. I sure wish I were there talking with you now. I could just hug you to death if I were there. If we have any trouble we will try to solve the problem first by talking it over with each other only in a good way. We don't ever have to worry about anything coming between us as we love each other too much to ever be apart from each other. You see now you are my wife and I don't want anything to take that away from me. I don't want anything to come and spoil it for us.

I know we were meant for each other or we would not have come together like we did. I am trying to tell you that I want you to be my wife the rest of my life no matter what happens. I promise you I will not do anything to cause you not to love me. I will never step out on you or say anything about you or smart mouth you ever or anything else that will cause you hurt. If I do, it will be because I didn't know about it. If I ever do anything like that let me know so I can make it right. Honey, we have to promise each other that we will love each other as much as the day we got married. I know I will you and maybe even more if that is possible. I will always do what it takes to make you proud to be my wife.

Honey, how are our children? Are they well? Do they remember me? Do you think they will like me when we are together for life? I will always be proud of them just as you would be if they were one of mine and yours. I promise with all my heart because that is the way God wants it to be and I know they would not want me as their father if I didn't. Darling, you know I owe Jr. a lot. Remember him on the bus? He was the one that got our conversation started when he said you weren't married anymore. That is one bus ride I will always remember. I will never forget putting my arms around you and kissing you for the first time. I sure wish I could be kissing you now.

It is twenty-four hours later now and it sure is dreary here now. I suppose you are moved by now. I wish I was home so we could move somewhere by ourselves. I got a letter from my Uncle Earl. That is my Aunt Agnes's husband. He is full of the devil. He was in the last war and he says that after that long, his wife still puts him on K.P.

Say, can you make a cackle berry pie. Or a wortail pie I can't but I do like gooseberry? Hah! I guess I will be on pastry detail next week. I think I will try to make some of those pies.

I can't think of much to write. Do you get my letters? I got a letter from my sis. I guess she is looking for her party before too very long. I hopes she gets along alright.

I guess I had better sign off now, but before I do, I would like to have a pass from you. Could I have it if I were there? Could I have it now? Well, Darling, I had better close for now. Remember I will always love you. So be good and I will do the same.

Your husband, Charles SWAK SWAK SWAK

P.S. Darling I love you more than anything else in the world.

To The Sweetest Girl God has Ever Given to Anyone,
To My Sweetheart,

Well, here I am again. I don't know what to say. Maybe I can make something up as I go along. I wrote to my folks and asked them to write you more often. Maybe they will write you now. Honey, if you wrote me every time I write you, I guess I will keep busy. I write you every chance I get now. But I will try to write more often.

Here are some cards I've sent. You can keep them or use them, whatever you want. I rode the boat in the one picture. When I came home from my furlough, I had to cross the bay to get a train to Oakland, California. It is a ferry boat.

Did you get all my letters? But anyhow, I will try to write you more often. But I am like you, now. You are probably getting sick of hearing the same thing over and over.

Honey I wish we could be together for good. The war is not looking good now, but it can't last forever. I hope not anyway. Everyone is thinking it will be over in "43 but I don't know about that. I got a letter from my sis. She is okay.

I didn't go to the show like I figured I would this evening. I got your letter and thought maybe I had better answer it. I hope I get another letter this evening, as I would rather answer it than go to a show.

I got a kind of slow headache. I never had a headache very often. I guess I didn't have enough in it to ache. Honey, I sure wish I could be there with you now for a good loving. Do you think I could? I would try anyway. I just rolled a cigarette. Do you want a puff? Did you quit smoking like you said you were?

I guess I had better stop now and go to school, as it is my day to go. Boy, Darling, you don't know how I would like to see you. I wished we lived closer to each other. But maybe someday we can. I sure hope so. If I ever got to live with you, you could be sure I would never leave you again. I wouldn't join a sewing circle once I get out of here. Isn't that some way to talk? But Honey, I love you so much I don't want to be anywhere where you can't be with me.

Well, I just got back from school, so will finish this. What is Robert and Bill doing these days? Has Odell been called up yet? I hope not. As short as the country is on farmers, I think it is better off keeping farmers home. I guess the Americans don't seem to be doing too good over in Africa right now. But one can't believe all he reads.

You know I would like to be with you. Wouldn't life be wonderful now if we could? Tell the children I said hello.

From the one who love your dearly, Charles SWAK

To The Sweetest Girl I've Ever Known.

Cora Mae, I Love You,

Well, Honey, I guess I had better sign off or I mean I had better drop you a few lines. I haven't heard from you for two days now. I hope you are okay. I ain't wrote to that woman yet, but I will.

Say Honey, did you ever find your step-ins? I ain't seen anything of them but I wish I was where I could see the ones you are wearing. Don't you?

Well, today was my washday. I washed three pairs of overalls, three suits on underwear and some stockings. I'll be glad when I can say, "Honey, will you wash my dirty clothes? You will probably say, "Yes if you will help me." But I will always be glad to help you. Honey, do you think you will always be glad of my teasing you? I sure will be glad to get my furlough. Boy, I can hardly wait.

This coming Sunday is Easter. Wish we could spend it together. Maybe we could find some eggs. Are you going to have any for the children? I'll be thinking of you and hoping you and the children will have a good time. I will most likely be cooking a Sunday dinner out here instead. I wish I could be there with you instead. Well, Honey, my pen just ran out of ink and I don't have much more to say, so as always, say hello to everyone for me.

Goodbye & Good Luck,

Your husband, Charles W. Ward SWAK XOXO

I got to go take a shower now. I wish you was here to wash my back. Do you remember when you washed my face and my back? I do. Darling, I love you more than anything in this world. Tell our children hello for me.

SWAK. SWAK I love you, I love you

Darling, I love You More Than Anything Else In This World,

My Darling Wife, I Will Always Love Her,

I sure hope Louise gets over her sickness. But I can't make out what kind of root she ate. I hope she is okay by now.

I got a letter from my folks and they are looking for you in May, as that would be the best weather. Well, Honey, I sure hope we can both be there in May. If nothing happens, we will be.

Well I must close for now and I will say, as always I love you. I will save my foolishness for my furlough.

Your husband, Charles SWAK

P.S. I will still figure on meeting you in Van Wert if nothing changes.

Cora Mae Gregory + Charles W. Ward on day they met.
A dime store photo booth

Backrow Mom; Front row Jr., Betty + Louise

Dad in combat gear (partial)

Mom + Dad in California

Aunt Florence + Uncle El in Tennessee

Evie + Burt; Friends + they shared apartment

Steam engine used for steaming young tobacco plants. It's size + screaming, piercing whistle sent two little girls scurrying under the bed

Grandpa + Grandma Ward

Uncle Bill (Mom's brother)

Dad's sisters + nephews. Alice in vehicle. Skeet,
Nelson + Alan Cleveland standing.

Dad with his favorite animal

Left; Mom + Evie in California

Dad + some army buddies

Dad in a tent camp

Dad

Mom + Dad in California

Mom + Dad a few days before he left for overseas

L to R—Louise, Grandpa Gregory, Betty. Front—Jr in front. In back—family car that took anyone in reach + could fit in, stand on running boards or sit on front fenders, to the movies on Saturday after noon. Also to sell cream + eggs + buy what few supplies they needed.

Evie + Burt

Dad while in the calvary

To The Swellest Person on Earth, MY Wife, Cora Mae,

Well, I guess I had better write to you now, as I won't be able to write tomorrow or the next day. I am going on another overnight trip.

Honey, I told my folks we would be there the 23rd or 24th. So don't let me down. I hope to meet you in Van Wert as I said in my last letter. And, if not there, then at my folks place.

Everything here is as usual. How is everything back there? Okay I hope. I have heard I am up for a corporal rating. My chances of getting it is pretty slim. I just don't think your husband is a very good soldier. But I never give up hope.

Honey, tell Robert I think he has a pretty wife. But I wouldn't trade him his wife for mine for a million dollars to boot. Boy, we will sure have a good time on my furlough. I hope nothing happens to stop it. Darling I love you more than anything else in this world. I'll bet we will have fun with your brothers and their wives. Honey, do they tease you because you have a soldier for a husband. That would not be very nice, would it?

I think we should spend half the time with my folks and half with your folks. Do you think that is fair? Let me know.

We will let them know what love is when I get there. Boy I sure am anxious to get there. I could only write foolishness, but I will wait until we are together and I will show you. I probably will be like a little boy with a new play wagon.

Darling I will close, dreaming of you night and day.

Your husband, Charles

To The One I Love,

Just to write to let you know everything here is okay as usual. I haven't heard from you for three or four days. Hope you are okay. I will be signing for my furlough in a few days. Hope you will be able to meet me as we planned. Hopes it meet with your approval, too. Boy, I am anxious to start home. We should have a swell time like we always do when we are together.

We had maneuvers last week. It didn't amount to much. We also got a prisoner in our group. One of the boys got tangled up in a net and we captured him, so he is our prisoner of war for now. We are giving him a hard time. He can't eat inside, only outside with an armed guard all the time. He will come out okay in the end.

I wish you could be out here. We sure could have a swell time. I guess when I come back from my furlough, I will be stationed two hundred fifty miles from this post to cook for an outpost. I hope so anyway.

I hope you have sent the money by the time you get this. If not, it will be too late. I hope by now, having you meet me in Van Wert did not make you mad.

How is everyone down there? You know I wrote that colored lady and she wrote back. I haven't answered yet but I will. She sure talks very nice of my wife and I am glad.

It is only seven days before my furlough. That seems a long time. I just can't hardly wait until I hold you in my arms. That will be a great day, won't it?

Well, I had better close and do my washing. Honey, tell the children I said hello and give them my love and that I will be seeing them before very long. Tell my wife that I love her dearly or does she know it by now?

I love you, honest I do.

Your husband, Charles

To The One I Love,

Dearest Wife,

Well another line to say hello and that everything here is okay. Probably by the time you get this, you will be all set to go to Ohio. I hope so anyway.

Everything is okay on the furlough. I received your letter of the 4th and glad to know you are okay. Well, I ain't going to the Mexican border. The transfer misfired. It don't matter how often you ask for a furlough, you are only going to get one every six months, anyway.

I didn't get to listen to the Grand Ole Opry because our radio was out of commission.

Honey I got a letter from my Aunt Agnes and she wants us to be sure and spend a night with them. She said it didn't matter if we got the bedclothes dirty, as they would wash.

But I don't think we will have time to spend a night there but we may be able to see them. I wrote home and told my folks that if anyone wanted to see us to have them come to their place. And you could tell your folks to do the same. Then we won't have to cut our time with each other short with our folks by traveling all over to see everyone. I suppose you think this is ugly of me, but you see, it will mean more time for each other. I really am trying to work out things that way.

When you receive this and you have not sent the money, then you ought to send it by telegraph. I've got to have the money by the 18th and if it doesn't get here I will be in a fix. But no matter, I will see you in Van Wert on the 22nd or 23rd.

Honey, I'll save my foolishness until I get there. So until then, remember that I love you.

SWAK

To The Most Precious Person to Me, Cora Mae, I Love You

Well Honey, I signed my furlough just now. I also got your letter and money order. I'll have to go to town now and get it cashed. So if nothing goes wrong, I am on my way home, soon. Boy, I can hardly wait to get there. I leave here on the 19th and shouldn't be over three days in getting there. So I should be in Van Wert sometime on the 23rd, day or night.

I got both of your letters. I sure was glad to get them, too. We had a boy to drown in our outfit. He was in a boat and an amphibious boat came too close to him and upset him and he couldn't swim. Boy that is tough luck. Some mother is going to have her heart broken. He has been in here as long as I have. But things like that happens, I guess.

Honey, you had better be set to get a good loving when I get there. I hope you can put up with me for a week.

Say hello to our family for me and everyone else. So this will be the last time I'll write till we meet. God be with you & the children.

Your husband, Charles

June

To The One I Love, Cora Mae,

Well, darling, I am back in camp after working for the day. I got here at ten o'clock last night and went back to work at six o'clock this morning. I was twenty four hours late but they didn't say anything about it. And, Honey, I had a surprise. I just found out I got a corporal's rating three days before I left for my furlough. That will give us a little more money and as time goes on maybe I will get an even better rating, which will mean even more money.

Darling, did you get that telegram I sent on my way back? Honey, I go on my transfer tomorrow but my address will stay the same. The more I think of it, the more I think of having you come out here. I can't stand being away from you anymore. It might be the best for both of us if we could be together. I would be a million times happier if you were here with me. I would have a better chance of showing you how it would be like if we were together all the time instead of only for a few days at a time. My love for you is true.

When I get to my new station, I will look around and see what I can make out for you to live here. It is just killing my whole soul having to be away from you. And if anyway is possible, I ain't going to be away from you anymore if I can help it. We only live once and it is so short a life, we had better be together all we can. See what you think about it.

If I stay out here another six months I believe all that is human in me would leave, You could find out how much it would cost to get someone to take care of the children. Your folks could if it would not be too much for them. Could you ask them and let me know? I would be forever grateful if they could.

Well Darling, I must close. It is mealtime and I am hungry. Hungry for you I might add.

Love forever and ever, Charles W. Ward

P.S. See what you think about it.

1943

To My One & Only,

Hi Honey,

I received your letter today and was very proud to get it. I'm glad you got the card. I don't think you have to send the checks to me to endorse. I made all the checks payable to you.

I wish I were there in bed with you. Only you would probably wind up kicking me out. Or, would you? I assure you there is no one I would rather sleep with than you. Honey, you will never know what it meant to sleep with you the week we were together. I had never slept with a woman before and I never knew how nice it could be.

Where did the card come from? Honey, have you heard from my folks lately? Darling, tell Bill I appreciate him looking out for my wife. I hope I can be there soon and look after you myself. I know if I were there now, we would be in bed together and better yet if it was raining. I would probably be in bed with you all day, raining or not. There isn't anyplace I would rather be, would you?

Honey, my idea of this war is that it will be over in the longest, two years. I sure hope so anyway. More than anyone knows. I sure hope that bird knew what it was doing when it built that nest in that gun. You tell the boys that are laying in bed is how lots of little juniors get on the way. But anyway, I wish I could be in bed with you, too.

Tell your folks to write to me. I wrote them but haven't heard back. Are they sore at me? God only knows I want to do right by you and them. Does your mother ever say anything about us being married? Would they rather you had married someone not in the army? Or do they say anything at all. Or is that any of our business?

Well, Darling, I must close and get back to work. It is Sunday here and has been raining all day. Hope it is nicer there. Maybe your dad needed the mare more than the saddle horse. The mare can pull a plow better than a saddle horse.

Honey, how are you and the one who tried to make trouble for you? Hope they ain't bothering you still. Boy, I am looking forward to being with you. The sun sure would shine then for me then. I imagine a lot of people will be glad when this war is over. And the sun shines for them, too. I wish I could be there now to hold you in my arms. And Honey, I love you with all my heart and soul. You can't imagine how I long for one of your kisses. More than you'll ever know. So I'll say that I love you.

Well, I got to close. Just know how happy I am to have you as my wife and in my life. Keep your chin up and everything will come out right. Give the children my love and I'll say so long,

From your devoted husband, Charles SWAK Answer soon

To The Sweetest One I Know, Cora Mae.

To My Darling Wife, Cora Mae,

Honey, I miss you terrible and love you more than ever. I got both your letters as of June 1st and 3rd. Boy, I was hoping for some word from you. I began to think you weren't going to write. Honey I sent a telegraph when I got in San Francisco. Did you get it? I can't think of anything you could do to make me any happier than I am now. Except to figure out a way for us to be together all the time. I love my wife very dearly.

About me not drinking or gambling. I'll make this deal. I won't drink or gamble any more if you make me this promise. Never to say that you are not good enough for me. If you promise me that then I will promise the other.

Honey, are you going to arrange things so you can come out here soon. I think my wife is a very brave woman and I love her dearly just for her being just the way she is. My folks told me in a letter that they thought you were swell, so we are bound to be happy together. I hope our Father in heaven will help guide us on the right road.

Darling, I hope you can fix things so you can come out here as soon as you can. You can sure enjoy it out here and I will be happy to have you near me. The ocean is about two hundred feet from the kitchen from where I work. We won't get another chance like this and I think we ought to take advantage of the situation. About the baby. You know I want one as bad as you, but I only want to be with you when you are out here. Don't forget how I got you "caught up" when I was home. Anything of you that has you in it, I love from the bottom of my heart and my soul. I pray for the day when I can be there to stay. I must close for now so I can shower and shave. Never forget my true love for you.

Tell our children hello for me and give Louise and Betty some sugar for me. Please write often and I promise the same.

Bye, Bye,

I Love you, Charles SWAK

July 1943,

To My darling Wife, I Love You,

Well another day has gone by. It sure is a nice day here. I guess we are going to get some new men in our outfit. Everything is as usual. No news, which makes writing about anything pretty scarce.

I hope you have gotten some of my letters that I wrote you by now. Have you received Mom's present yet? Did you like it?

You said that you had almost quit smoking. Honey, if you want to smoke that is okay. It makes no difference to me. You do as you want. The only thing is that it would be better for you if you did quit. But if it helps you any to smoke, go ahead. I will love you no matter what you do.

You know, it is funny, but a few of the boys around here seem to be interested in you. Every once in a while one of them will ask how my wife is doing. They seem to want my wife to be okay. While we were eating dinner one day, one of them asked me how Cora Mae was doing? I told him "fat and sassy, I hope." Haha. One guy asked why I got married and I told him because I loved you. He told me I didn't have enough heart enough to love any one. What do you think of that? Well, maybe I don't have a heart but I've got a good wife and she will just have to put up with me.

I sure hope we can be together soon, sometime in the near future. Forever and then some. I sure spend a lot of time thinking about you. It is the only thing I get pleasure from.

Well, I can't think of much more to say so I will close and try writing a letter to your folks. Darling, remember I love and worship you. Answer soon.

Your husband, Charles

P.S. SWAK I LOVE YOU. I sure liked those pictures. I will keep them always.

Cora Mae, My Darling,

Well Honey, I write you again. I am going to try to write you one letter everyday. But if I miss every once in awhile, you can say, "Well he didn't have time today". I am sitting in our kitchen while writing this. I can look right out over the ocean while sitting at the kitchen table. It is only about two hundred feet from the edge of the water.

I wish you could come out here to see it as well as the rest of the country out here. You would never forget it. Then we could be together for a while. That is why I am so anxious for you to come out here so we could be close and we could see this country together. You would like it, I think. There ain't no telling though how long we will be here as they could ship us out any time. I won't draw no pay for another month, but we could do it someway if you came out here.

How are the children coming along? And how is little Junior doing or is there going to be one? I am anxious to know. How is Bill & Polly getting along? Tell them I said hello. They sure were nice to me while I was there.

I asked about the gas rationing tickets I was suppose to have got. I was suppose to go to the stationary board where I lived and get the tickets. I'll know better next time. Did you get your check this month? I hope so.

I want you to write often and let me know how everything is by you. How did you make out on that gravestone for Shirley? Write me about everything because I want to share your thoughts or worries about everything, all I can. Don't hold back on anything on account of thinking it would make me feel bad. Your business and troubles are mine too, now.

How are your folks getting along? Tell them I said hello. I wish you would tell your mother that I thank her for giving me such a sweet wife.

I guess I can't think of much else to say at this time so from one who loves you dearly I must close. I hope I acted enough like a husband when I was with you to make you know I love you with all my heart and soul. I started this letter yesterday but missed the mail call so I will mail it today. I hope this finds you well.

You are loved dearly,

Your husband, Charles SWAK

To The Sweetest One I Love and the Swellest Wife I Know,

Dearest Wife,

Well, here it is. Another week has gone by and everything is the same. I was fishing at the beach but didn't get a nibble. I picked up some sea shells and will send them to you as soon as I can get to it. You can give Aunt Florence some of them. You can tell her they are from the windy shores of the Pacific Ocean.

I had a pretty good dream of you last night. Boy I wish it would come true. I've been thinking it over wondering if you would feel any different or if I would feel any different since I was home for my furlough. Honey, I don't feel any different. Do you? Only that I love you more. I know how you think I feel but Honey, I don't. All I can say is that I love you more than anything in this world. I am very proud of my wife and I love her dearly. I wouldn't trade my married life for a single life as long as you are my wife. Honey, I wouldn't ever regret marrying you if I lived to be a million years old. There is no use of you worrying about me not loving you, as that can never be. I'll always love you no matter what and I will always wish you were here with me. I will really be happy when this war is over. Me and you are really going to be happy, won't we? Can't think of anything I would rather do except be beside you all the time.

Well, Honey, I must close and go to bed. I'll write more to this tomorrow and send it out at noon tomorrow as the mail only goes out once a day. So Honey I'll say goodnight. How are our children doing?

Well, here I am again. This morning I bought some cards and I will send them out to you so you can see how my life looks like out here. People are fishing on the beach but I don't know if they are catching anything or not. It sure gets cool here in the mornings.

I Love you.

Your husband, Charles. SWAK

Cora Mae, My Darling,

Well, I write you again. How I wish you were here. You would really enjoy yourself out here. There has been a hundred girls out here on the beach today. They really have a time.

Well, supper is close now, so I had better stop for now. I will finish in the morning.

It is Monday morning so I will finish this letter so I can get it out in the mail, today. It is a nice day on the beach. There are many guys out there fishing today. Honey, I am looking for a letter from you today.

So, Darling, don't forget to write and I will do the same. I'll write you again tomorrow. I am going to try to write everyday and I hope you can do the same. So for now, I will say so long and good luck. Tell everyone I said hello.

Your loving husband, Charles

I love you. Honest I do. SWAK

To the Sweetest Girl I Know,

Cora Mae, I love you,

Well, I guess I will write a little, while I got time. Tonight we are having swiss steak and baked beans. A pretty easy menu. I didn't hear from you today. Maybe tomorrow. How are you? I am okay, only lonely for my sweet wife. You know how that is.

How is Bill & Polly? I wish I were there so we could sit side by side to eat supper. We sure would be set, wouldn't we? We would be happy anyhow.

I wrote Aunt Florence and Uncle El a letter. I hope it won't be long before we are together again for good. I know I sound like a broken record, but what else can I say when it is true. Have you given Jr. any spankings? Has your Dad given you any? Haha. I guess I will write and tell him to give you one for good luck.

I wish you could see the ocean out here today. The waves are fine. I wish you were here so you could see this country. We may never get a chance like this again.

Have you heard from my folks yet? Say, did they send that ice box to you? If not, do you think you would like to have it?

I think I will stop for awhile and finish this letter after supper.

Well, supper is over and I just received your letter of the 7th and was very glad to get it. I am glad you got my telegram okay. Honey, I always fall more in love with you and am anxious to be with you again. I wish you would forget about me not being satisfied with you. You couldn't make me any more happy and proud to have you as my wife than you do already. I am not just saying that. I mean it with all my heart and would not kid you about a thing like that. I don't feel any different since I came back to camp, only that I love you more each time I see you. So, please Darling, don't think I am kidding about that. Remember what you promised.

It is okay about the baby. It wouldn't be fair to you when you are alone. When that happens, I want you to be there all the time and when I am able to be with you, as I should be. I sure hope, too, that nothing goes wrong in our married life. I will do everything I can to keep things from going wrong. Honey, if anything ever happens to us my life won't be worth a penny because my wife is all I live for. God in heaven knows I truly love her. Darling, you've got to promise not to let anything come between us until I can get out of the army. Then, I can have my equal chance to prove I love you truly. There is difference in my love since I came back. I am even more lonely. I learn to love you just that much more.

So I will close, hoping to hear from you soon. So bye, bye. I love you forever, honest.

Your husband, Charles

1943

Dear Mother,

How are you getting along? Fine I hope. Myself, okay. I say hello to you Mother and Daddy. Mother I want a drum for a present. Dad, how is the army getting along? Fine I hope.

Mother, I haven't missed a day in school yet and Daddy Williams gave me an airplane hat for my birthday. Martha is writing a letter to you and I am writing a letter to you too. I write down hill.

I am going to write again and am okay for the present. Answer soon in a long letter. Happy to see you soon.

I am happy,

Your son, JR

BOOK THREE

Overseas

Sept. 10th, 1944

Well darling, I am back in camp. I am missing you at not being able to be with you. Seems funny not having you standing here by my side. It is like there is an empty space here beside me. But Darling, maybe it won't be long until we are together for good.

I hope this finds you okay and our home all set up. Honey, I did hate to go off and leave you like that, I just couldn't help it. Your folks all seemed to be so far away from you in the last two days we were together. I think, Honey, they resented us coming in like we did. I don't think they like the way we want to do things. But don't worry, we will be on top when all is said and done. So Darling, just do the best you can and get along as you can and when we can be together to stay, we can do as we like and be happy in our own way.

When you get this, answer real soon, as I will be waiting to hear from you. Write and tell me how you are making out in Ohio. Tell me everything, how you did, how you made the trip up from Tennessee. How did you get to the train station when you started? Did someone take you there? What are you making out for a living room suite? Have you got one yet? Or are you getting one? Are you going to get the one we looked at? Do the children like Ohio? Boy, I can ask more questions than you can start to answer.

Honey, about you coming back out here to see me. That would be nice but as things are now, it can't be. Things are not so good, if you know what I mean. And I guess you do. If the time comes, you can be sure I will let you know.

Boy, Honey, I'll be glad when I can come home to stay. I will lay in bed on a cold winter morning while you make a fire and cook me breakfast and serve it in bed. Oh boy!! Won't that be something? I can just see that, can't you? Haha.

Honey, I may try to call you one of these days, but not just yet. Maybe in a week or ten days or so. I will let you know later but I will have to reverse the charges. But, Honey, I will try to write everyday as long as I can and you do the same.

How did you and the folks make out? They really keep tabs on you, I suppose. You will really hate me from now on, I reckon. All I care is that you love me like I love you and everything will be alright.

Well, Honey, I will close for now and hope you are well and okay. I love you with all my heart and soul.

Answer soon, your husband, Charles

1944

Dear Folks

Just a few lines to let you know I am okay. Hope this finds you all okay. Sure seen lots of water. I only got sick a couple of times. Have you heard from Jim yet? This letter is intended for my wife. I am using your address so I can be sure she gets it.

Boy, I only want to cross the ocean one more time and that is when I come back. There is sure too much water to drink if I should fall overboard. Tell my wife I said hello and that I love and think of her everyday.

Be sure and give her this letter and tell her I am okay. I will write to her soon. Tell her also that I love her very much. So I will close. Write often and tell me all the news and what is going on.

So Long and Good Luck

Cora Mae, I Love You Very Much,

Well, Honey, I received your letter today, the first in three days. I will answer it now. I am glad the folks are getting along good in their work. I wish I were there to help. I use to get a lot of enjoyment of working horses with a plow, although, it does tire my legs.

Honey, I don't mistrust you of stepping out on me. I just trust you too much to even think of that.

The pictures should come along with the letter. I sent them at the same time. I got a letter from my sis. She said she had gotten a letter from you. She also said my pop was waiting for the day when I come back and start farming with him. Honey, I don't hardly know what to think.

You are probably still asleep back there. There is just about five hours difference between here and there. So, that would make it five o'clock there. I can see you lying in bed now.

How are the kids coming along? Fine I hope. Everything here is okay. Hope everything is okay with you all, too. Honey, I wish I could just sit and watch you take a bath. I would get a kick out of that. Probably in the behind, too, I bet. Haha

Well, Darling, I can't think of much else to write, so I'll close and write another letter to my sis. So keep writing as your letters mean a lot to me. I'll close saying I love you very much and dearly and God bless you and our children. So until we meet again, answer soon.

Your husband, Charles

Answer soon & often. SWAK

England

Dearest Darling,

Well Honey, just a few more lines today. I got your letter of October 22nd. I am glad you are all okay.

I am sure sorry about your wallpaper coming off. Maybe you will have better luck next time. I would like to have been there to play ball with you and the kids. That would have been the best fun I had since I left you. I sure would be glad to be home to play ball or just be alone with you. That will sure be a great day for me and lots of other guys, as well. I know it is something we all would appreciate greatly.

Boy Honey, you will never know what a great place Ohio is until you get away from it, like I am. Anyplace in the U.S.A. would be good to me now.

Well Honey, I am out of air again so I will close saying I love you dearly. Keep writing and I will do the same.

From your husband, Charles

God Bless You

Dearest Darling,

I got your letter of October 15. I am glad I finally got it. I am also glad you all got the soybeans in. I wish I could have been there to help. I'll bet Dad was happy to get them in too. Do you like doing soybeans? Tennessee farmers do not grow them but Ohio farmers do not grow tobacco. Not in our part of the country anyway.

By the way, you have never said what you did on the combine. What did you do? What are you doing now? You've got to be careful on those machines and not get tangled up in them. Have you got so you can drive your car good? One thing for sure, I will have a chauffer waiting for me when I get home. Haha

I hope you got your radio okay.

So I will close saying I love you dearly. Be sure to write often. Tell everyone I said hello. Love & Best Wishes

Dearest Darling,

Just a few lines to let you know I am okay and all is well. I got the pictures and was proud to get them. I am glad you sent them. I look at them everyday.

Today is Saturday and not much work, so I took the time off to write to you. I'll write another one tonight. I hope you are getting my mail. I got a letter from Mom & Dad Ward. They sure talk good of you. Honey, I sure miss being around you. It seems funny to be so far apart. It is not right. But, Darling, I don't think the war can go on much longer. I hope not anyway.

Well, I had better close saying I love you. So until we meet again,

Your husband, Charles

Dearest Darling,

Well, Honey, just a few lines to let you know I am okay and hope this finds you the same. I am glad you got my letters and also glad you heard from my brother Jim.

About those boys you asked me about. They are both over here with me so you won't have to worry as much. How do you like your heater by now? How are the children coming along?

I don't know how the Wards ever got along without you either. Not bragging are you? Now don't work too hard. You know even a good horse can wear out after awhile. So don't forget that.

I am glad you didn't send me anything for my birthday. I spent my birthday out on the ocean someplace on a ship someplace. Nice way for me to spend it. Sure wish I could have spent it with you and the children. With God's help we will spend it together sometime. Wouldn't that be nice?

Will close for now. Love & Best Wishes,

Your husband, Charles

Dearest Darling,

Well Honey, just a few lines to let you know I am well and okay. Hope this finds you the same. Sure is a nice day in Europe for a change.

How is your washer? How is your mother? Let me know things like that. I sure wish I were there. How are you getting along? I hope you got your house set up. Only, I wish we were living in it together. How are the children? Does Louise like school? I'll bet she is a pill just like her mother is a pill.

Have you met any of the folks there yet? If so, what do you think of them? Have you gone to church, yet?

Well, Honey I can't think of much else to say at this time. I will say a prayer for you and the children every night.

Goodbye & God Bless you,

Did you get your coal or not? Coal may be hard to get at this time.

Well, Honey, keep your chin up and I love you.

Your husband, Charles,

Dearest Darling,

I got five letters from you this evening. I sure was glad to get them. You know, I write to you everyday. You will probably get them as I get yours . . . all bunched up. Anyway I get them is alright with me as long as I get them. I know what it is like not to get any mail.

Honey, I didn't like that remark about the cider and your head spinning. I hope I don't have anything to worry about. If that stuff affects you like that, why drink it? I guess I will have to get me some cider and make my head spin.

Well, ain't much to say.

God Bless You, Charles

Dearest Darling,

Just a few lines to let you know everything is okay. It rained here for a change. Haha. Oh to be back there in Paulding County for awhile. What did you think of the fair or did you go? Are the folks done with the beans? What made your wall paper come off anyway? Did the roof leak or what? Did they get it fixed or not?

Well Sweetheart, how are the children coming along in school? How do you like Ohio? Are you as satisfied as you were in Tennessee? Just tell me how and what do you think of the place? Don't beat around the bush. Let me now for true.

Also, what did Roy think when he was there? Write and tell me.

Well, hoping to hear from you soon.

Love and God Bless you, Charles

Dearest Darling,

Just a few lines to let you know I am okay. I got three letters from you the other day. Two were airmailed and one by v-mail. Boy was I glad to get them. I hope you are getting mine okay. I write two letters a day. Not much to write though. I just feel closer to you when I do.

I am glad you are getting along good. I wish I was there to eat supper with you. I would help you wax the floors, too. I hope you get your cow. How do you like Alice for a companion. Does she give you any trouble? Boy, sweetheart, I sure do miss you and the others. I wish we could be together all the time.

I hope you haven't forgotten what happened two years ago on the ninth day of November. Do you remember? I do and will never forget.

Well, I will close with love and best wishes.

Your husband, Charles

My Darling Wife,

Well I hope this finds you all okay. I am. Everything here is as usual.

Have you heard anything from your folks back in Tennessee since you were there? If so, how are they? What are you doing these days? Are you working out in the cold? Honey, I don't want you to. So I hope you won't. Take care of yourself and the children.

I am glad you are straight at the bank now. I bet you are glad too. Have you got your cow back yet? How do your stoves work? Does that cook stove bake or not? Was that door sprung or not? Did they fix it so it would stay shut or what? How did you ever came out with that paper that fell off the wall after you put it on?

Honey, I wish I was there to help you instead of over here where I can do you no good. Then I wouldn't have to ask so many questions. That would so much better, wouldn't it? I sure think so anyway.

Well Honey, I hope you can answer all my questions. How are the folks? All well I hope. Tell them hello for me. God bless you and keep you for me. I love you dearly.

Your husband, Charles SWAK

Dearest Darling,

I ain't got nothing to do so I will write a few more lines to you today. I sure am lonesome and dreary today.

Honey, are much of my letters censored out when you get them? How are the children doing? I would give a lot if I could be with you and them again. That will be a great day for me and I hope for you all as well when we can all be together again.

How do they like it up there by now? Do they get homesick? Did you have any trouble getting them on the right track again? Pretty hard on you, I bet. I wish you had me there to start out again. Do you think you could do that? I bet you would give it a try, wouldn't you?

Well Darling, I guess I will close. Not much news I can talk about. So keep the letters coming and I will do the same.

From the one who loves you dearly. Tell all I said hello and to write to me. You write and tell me about yourself and how you are coming along.

Your husband, Charles

Dearest Darling,

Well Honey, just a few lines to say hello and say that everything here is okay.

It is Thanksgiving Day and we are having turkey and all the trimmings. But I still haven't got a letter from you. Sure seems funny that I am not getting any letters from you. All the other fellows are getting letters from their wives and it makes me feel very unhappy. But believe me if I try real hard I will get along.

How are you folks doing by now. What are you having for Thanksgiving dinner?

Well there ain't much I can write. Only lots of questions as there ain't no letters to respond to.

How are the children coming along? Fine I hope.

Well, Honey, I will write again when I get a letter to respond to so I will close saying

God Bless you, Charles

Dear Little Ladies, (Betty & Louise)

Well what are you doing now? I bet playing in the snow. I wish your daddy could be there. I would throw snowballs at you, Haha. How are you doing with your mom these days? Are you keeping warm? How do you like your grandpa and grandma in Ohio? Do they give you spankings? I'll bet they do. I would give you both a spanking when I get there. I am going to chew Betty's ear off too when I get home. Are you girls being good for your mom? Now, you take care of her and keep her out of the cold while I am away.

So God Bless you & keep you for me,

Daddy Charles

Love & Kisses

My Darling Wife,

How are you getting along? Have you got enough money or not? Are you getting that forty dollars you are suppose to get each month? I will draw about forty dollars a month over here but there is nothing to spend money for. I will probably send most of it to you. I'm not sure yet.

Boy, I'm not sure I like this country over here. I wish they would give England to the Indians. How do the children like school? Tell them I said hello. Tell our baby (Betty) to write more often. Her writing ain't so plain but I can read it. How is she anyway? I would like to see them all and their mother too. Honey, how do you like it up there by now? Do you ever hear from your ex-husband? Do you have enough money or not?

The boys are eating supper now, so according to that it should be eleven o'clock back there where you are. How do you and Mom get along now? Do you have any arguments? I hope not. Well I can't thing of much else to say so I will close until tomorrow. So for now I will see about eating some supper. I wish I were there eating with you and the children.

I will say I love you, good night, so long and good luck. Answer soon.

Your husband, Charles

Dearest Darling Wife,

Well, I will try to write you a few lines. You can tell the folks you got a letter from me. I hope you are all okay. I am just fine. But I suppose I could be better. I'm still waiting to come home. Most everyone could be better over her just now.

How are the folks coming along? Hope they are all well. How are the children doing? Are they going to school everyday? Has it got cold there yet?

Boy, I bet you are all having a good time back there. Sure would like to be there to help. How does your house look? I bet it sure is pretty.

Well, Honey, for once it is a nice day here, sunny and bright. Are you living in your house now or are you still with the folks?

I can't think of much else to say, only that I love you. I don't like it here. Haha. Some joke! Well, I had better sign off for now, so be good and be careful until we are back together again.

Your husband, Charles

Well, I just got through sewing some stripes on my uniform. It sure made my fingers sore. I wish I had you here to sew them on for me. I promise I won't lose these stripes as I did before when we were in the states. You sure got tired of sewing them on, time after time, didn't you? Haha. I love you. Give the children my love. Tell my folks hello and to write me. Answer soon.

Dearest Darling,

Well Honey, just a few lines to let you know I am okay and well and to answer your letter that I received yesterday. Boy I sure was glad to hear from you. I am glad you are okay and well. You can do just as you please at Christmas. Just remember it can be dangerous and crowded, traveling over the holidays. But you do as you think best but be careful.

I got three letters from Sis today. She said Mom and Dad thinks the world of you and the children. Boy Honey, that sure means a lot to me. I hope they always will think well of you and the children.

Everything here is pretty good. I love you more than anything else in this world and I hope you can say as much for me. Can you?

There ain't no news of any kind that I can talk about anyway. I just pray Darling that we can spend the next Christmas together. I ain't spent a Christmas home for three years now. But now, I have more reason to want to.

Well, Darling, I will close saying I love you and our children. So God bless you all.

Your husband, Charles

My Darling Wife, Cora Mae

Well, Honey, just a few lines to let you know all is well with me. How are you and your folks? Fine and dandy I hope. I am doing okay, just very lonesome for my wife. There is no news. Just the usual.

Honey, I'll never forget the words you said to me when I left. Boy, that was fine of you. I hope we never have to part again. How are the children? Give them each a hug and kiss for me. Be sure to take real good care of them. Take good care of yourself as well.

Honey, how do you like it up there now? Have you got your cow yet? Be sure and drink plenty of milk so you will be fat like you were when we parted. Don't you worry over me. Everything will turn out okay. It always has, hasn't it? If we trust in our Lord, it always will. Honey, don't smoke too many cigarettes. They are not good for a person.

And don't forget, if anything goes wrong be sure to let me know. Tell me the truth always about anything. And I mean anything. Remember, we promised never to fib to one another. If anyone mistreats you, be sure to let me know. Because I worry and wonder how you are getting along all the time.

Well, I can't think of much else to say. From the one who loves you more than anything else in the world.

Your husband, Charles

P.S. Let me know when you get your mailbox up and I will send your mail direct to you. Bye for now, Sweetheart. SWAK SWAK XOXO

Dear Louise, Betty & Jr.

Just a few lines to let you know your Daddy ain't forgotten you. I write your mother everyday and often two times a day, so I will write you kids a few lines now. Tell Mama your Daddy says that he hoped that you all have a good Christmas and that he wishes he could be there with you. He said he would make it up when he can.

Are you children going to school everyday now? I love you but would spank you if you don't. How do you like going to school there? How do you get along with your grandpa and grandma? Do you help Mother with her work? Do everything you can to help her. And if she does too much, give her a whipping for me.

That is about all I can say for now, so you write to me and tell me all about yourself. Bye and be good for me.

Your Daddy,

Bye for now.

Honey, don't forget to date your letters and write often, Answer soon. I love you, Charles.

Dearest Darling,

I hope this finds you all okay. It leaves me fine and well. Be sure and use the latest address on the last letter you get each time. Things keep changing all the time. They keep us coming and going.

How does this find you? Fine I hope. How are the children? Sure would like to be with you and them. Does Jr. like school? Is he coming along okay? How is Betty and Louise. Give them my love and tell them I would like to see them and their mother.

Well, Honey, I will close for now, so be good.

God bless you and keep sending me letters and answer soon. As many as you can. I look for them every day.

Love, Charles

Dearest Darling Wife,

Just a few lines to let you know all is okay by me. I hope you got my other letters okay and that you use the P.O. that is on my return address. How is everything by you now? How are you coming along by now? I wrote to your folks. Have you heard from them? How are the children? Have any of them got sick from the change in climate? How do they get along there? How is Dad getting along with his crops? Is he well? How are you and my baby brother getting along? Does he come and visit you? How are you furnished transportation to town or do you get to town? Have you got your check as you should or has it been delayed?

Well, Honey, I will close for now. So be good. So Long and God bless you. Hugs and kisses,

Your husband, Charles I love you.

Dearest Wife & Family,

Well, just a few lines this evening to let you know I am okay. I hope it finds you the same.

Tell Jr. I have answered his letter but will do so again so he will be sure to receive one of the letters. Honey I am lonesome for you and the children tonight. Boy I sure would enjoy being with you all. Would you? I bet so.

How is your cow and calf coming along? I hope they don't get sick on you. By the time we get together, you should be quite a hand at raising livestock. Haha

Well, my Darling, I can't find too much more to say just now so I will close this one and write more in the morning. So Honey, I will close saying I love you more than anything else in this world. So God Bless you and keep our children for us.

Tell my folks I said hello. Write and tell me all about yourself. How you are and how you are coming along.

From one who loves you dearly.
Your husband, Charles XOXO

Dearest Darling & Wife,

Well, Honey just a few lines to answer the letters I got from you today. I am glad you are okay and the children. Too.

Now Honey, you asked me if I loved you as much as I did. Now you know the answer to that without my saying it. But I still will tell you how I feel about it. To me there is no one on this earth to take your place with me. I love you with all my heart and look forward everyday when I can come back to you. And I will as fast as I can. You can bet your life on that. Now you see how I feel about you.

I hope this finds you and the children all okay and well. So God Bless you and give the children a kiss from me and tell them that I love them very much. Take good care of yourself,

Your husband, Charles XOXO

Dearest Darling,

Well, just a few lines to let you know I am okay and well. Hope this finds you the same.

Honey about those cigarettes. I am going to share them with some of the boys. I hope you don't mind. I knew you wouldn't. Haha

I don't have much to say except to say that I am dogtired and my feet and heart sure are aching for you and home. I am feeling okay otherwise. I sure would like to see you again. I sure would enjoy that. How are the children these days?

Honey, I got a letter from Sis. She didn't have much to say except there weren't much news and things were the same and she was alright. Have you heard from your folks lately or not? I haven't. Have you got your corn out yet? Is your cow giving good milk or not?

How are you getting along with your radio? Does it work good? Who went with you to get it? What kind of radio is it? And is it electric or battery or both? How are the folks making out? Is the weather such that they can work out on the farm? Or is the cold weather still hanging on? How are their cows getting along? Are they getting much milk?

Well, Honey, I've asked as many questions as I can think of. I will close saying God Bless you and the children. Tell everyone I said hello.

Love & Kisses,

Your husband, Charles

Dearest Darling,

Well, just a few lines to say hello and everything is fine and okay here. I hope this finds you the same or better. I got a letter from Sis the other day. She is doing fine but didn't have very much to say except she is lonely too.

Honey, I ain't heard from you for a week now. I sure am looking for a letter soon. Maybe yet, today. How are the kids coming along? Fine I hope. How are you by now? Are you well? I hope you ain't forgotten who I am. That is why I keep waiting to hear from you.

There ain't much for me to say and nothing to respond to. So I will close, saying so long and good luck.

Your husband, Charles

To the Sweetest Girl on Earth, My Wife Cora Mae,
Honey I miss you terrible.

Well another day has gone by and no letter from you. I sure do get down hearted when I don't get one. Now Honey, I don't mean to nag at you. I know the mail is very crowded on account of Christmas. I know I will get one eventually but I sure do miss it when I don't get one. Most of all I miss you.

I got a letter from Sis. She keeps telling me how much the folks think of you. They can't think any better of you than I do. Well I sure look forward to being with you again. That sure will be a happy day for me.

How are the children? Are they okay? Do they like their school?

Well, Sweetheart, I will close, as there isn't any news. I will say I love you dearly with all my heart. So God bless you and our children.

Love and Best Wishes,
Your husband, Charles

Dearest Darling,

Well Honey, just a few lines to let you know I got your letters and sure was glad to get them and know you were alright. I hope you still are when you receive this. I'm okay only lonesome for you. Boy, Honey I wish I were there to drink your coffee when your back was turned. But I wouldn't put any onions in it. Haha.

I received a letter from Aunt Florence telling me you had been down to see her. I also got Jr.'s letter. Well, honey, I wish I could be there and I sure would be happy if I was. Now you write me a nice long letter telling me all about yourself.

Yes, I suppose the children were a worry to travel with. I don't see how you could make a trip like that, but I am glad you made it.

Well, I must close, saying I love you more than anything else in the world. God Bless you and the children. Say hello to everyone for me.

So good night and good luck,
Your Husband

Dearest Darling,

Well, Honey, how does this find you? Well, I hope. It leaves me well. How are the children coming along? Are they well? I hope so.

Honey, I got your letter with the bank note in it. And I will return it soon. Glad you got it settled up.

I got a letter from Myle Gepheart today. It was wrote Thanksgiving Day. It sure took a long time to get here.

Honey, how are you these days? Are you well? I hope you are. Things are about the same here. No news of any kind.

Honey I sure would like to see you. I sure do get lonesome for you. How are my folks? Are they well? I haven't heard from Skeet lately. I guess her time is near. I hope she comes through okay. How are the children coming along in school?

My pen isn't any good as you can tell by my writing. So I love you.

God Bless You,
Charles XOXO

I feel that Dad's letters were getting quite cryptic and short because he was aware that his mail was quite possibly being censored and this affected his openness at this time.

Dearest Darling,

Well, Honey, I will write you and let you know your wife is okay and well. I hope you are the same. I am lonesome for you, as I didn't get a letter from you today. So I guess that is why I am lonesome for you.

Our kids are okay and well. It won't be too long until you come home to us. I hope so anyway.

Honey, our calf is okay. He runs around kicking up his heels at me, anyway. Haha

So my Darling, I wanted to tell my husband how much I love him. I'll close so I can get this in the mail today.

Your wife, who misses you very much and more than I can say.

Cora Mae

To the Sweetest Girl I know, My Wife, Cora Mae,

Well Honey, I thought I would sit down and write you a few lines. Everything here is okay and the same as it was. I hope you are okay and well and happy. I'm sure you and the children are coming along good in Ohio. I only regret I can't be there with you to help. I'll bet your folks blew sky high when you left. Did they seem so mad? After all I promised I would not take you away from there. But it could not be helped as I see it.

I am off now until two o'clock on Tuesday. I wish I could be there to spend that time with you. I just got my hair cut, took a shower and shaved. All ready to go and no place to go. No place I want to go to anyway. I would like to come home but they won't let me.

How about the roof? Did they get it fixed so it don't leak or will you have to wait until it rains to find out? How does the wood burn in the cook stove? Is it cold up there yet? I'll bet it is in the mornings. Do the children have enough warm clothes for the winter? Or do you have to get them yet? Be sure they get plenty of warm clothes.

Have you gone to town yet or are you afraid to go? You know those Ohioians will snap and bite. Haha. Or they might ask you for a date. Oh, oh!!

Well Sweetheart, I can't think of much more foolishment, as I ain't in that mood. I can think of something I am in the mood for though.

I love you like nobody's business and more than anything else in the world. So be good and be careful and don't take any wooden nickels.

God bless you, from one who loves you dearly,

Your husband, Charles XOXO

Dearest Darling,

I am writing another letter just now as I didn't get very much on the first one. The v-mail doesn't have much room on them to write much. Everything here is as usual.

Honey, I am sending you two v-mails and one by airmail. Now when you get them, check the date and see which one you got first and then write and tell me which way you want me to send my letters to you. V-mail or air mail. Either one is okay by me.

Boy, Honey, that tobacco your folks sent me sure was good. I was glad to get some of that kind of tobacco.

Well, Sweetheart, I had better sign off and hope this finds you okay. It leaves me alright. So God bless you and keep you for me. Tell our children I said hello and give them a big hug and kiss from me. I love you all with all my heart and soul.

Your husband, Charles XOXO

Dearest, Darling Wife,

Well, just a few lines to let you know that I am well as can be expected since I am so far away from you. Hope you are well also.

I imagine you are very busy, now, getting our home set up. How are you getting along with the people there? Have you visited Mrs. Ross since you have been there?

Did any of your folks get there for Christmas? Did the children like their presents? What are you all doing these days besides trying to keep warm. Do you go to church or not?

Honey, I sure do miss your letters so keep them coming. I hope to get a dozen of them today.

God Bless you my darling. Tell our children I love them very dearly and their mom too. Tell everyone I said hello and to write often.

I Love You,
Your husband, Charles XOXO

Dearest Wife,

Just a few lines to let you know I am okay. I hope it finds you the same. I haven't got any letters from you for two days now. I'll probably get a bunch of it soon. I hope so anyway.

How is everything back there now? I hope you got your radio okay. I only wish I could be there to listen to it with you. I sure have been lonesome and lovesick the last couple of days. What I wouldn't give to be home. It just can't be helped, I guess. I just hope this war ends before I get too old to live. I am beginning to feel old already. Haha. Anway it can't end too soon for me.

Honey, you never did say which room the wallpaper came off of. Has anymore come off or not? Does the roof still leak? How are the children? Tell them I said hello.

I'll close for now, saying I love you very dearly.

Your husband, Charles Answer soon and often

Dearest Wife & Family,

Well, Sweetheart, just a few lines to answer your letter that I received today of April 5th. It got here a lot quicker than I expected. I hope this leaves you well and okay. I am alright except I am lonely and yearning for you. The weather sure has been dreary lately.

Boy, it seems I get more homesick everyday. Instead of getting better, I get worse. They sure have nice horses over here. I would say comparable to the ones they have in Kentucky. Beautiful horses and fast women. Haha

They are about fifty years behind in the farming. They still use a lot of oxen to work their fields. Only wish they were that far behind in their warfare.

Well, Honey, I am about out of news so I will ask a few questions and close. How are the children? Okay I hope. Are you getting any garden in yet? Do you plan to? I saw a deer today but was too far away to shoot it. I guess we won't have any deer meat tonight. We had some the other day and it was good.

Well, Darling, I will close. God bless you and the children for me. From one who loves you dearly,

Your husband, Charles Answer, kisses, good luck and good night

Dearest Darling,

Well Honey, just a few more lines to let you know I am okay and well. I am on duty now and it is about 9:15 o'clock in the evening. But it isn't quite dark out yet. I hope this finds you all well.

How are those potatoes that you planted? Are they up yet? I hope you have good luck with them. How are your chickens? What kind did you get? Did Mom or Pop get any? If so, how many? How is Mom feeling these days? Sis wrote me some time ago and said Mom was having some kind of trouble. Mom wouldn't say anything of it to me even if I asked her. So will you try to find out and let me know?

Well, I had better get busy and start getting some grub ready for tomorrow morning or I will be in trouble.

God bless you and the children for me and keep you well and safe for me. Be sure and let me know about Mom, won't you?

From One Who Loves You Dearly and With All My Heart,

Your husband, Charles XOXO

Dearest Wife,

Well, Honey, just a few lines this evening to let you know all is well and okay with me. I sure hope you are the same if not better there.

I received the two cigarettes you got me. I was glad to get them, but the size of them gave me quite a surprise. Are they the size you are using? Should be good for a long smoke anyway. Haha.

Honey, I didn't get any letters. I hope you ain't forgot me. Have you? I ain't forgotten you. I never could forget you, even if I wanted to. Anyway I never want to.

Honey, how are the children coming along? Are they well? I've asked you this before but you have never answered me yet. Are you going to be able to send me some pictures of my wife and family? I know you have sent some and I still have them. But I want to see if you have growed any. I bet the children have.

Well, I am getting short on news so I will close. God bless you and our children. Be sure to take care of yourself and the children. Say hello to everyone there.

From one who loves you dearly,

Your husband, Charles Love & Kisses Answer soon

Dearest Wife,

Well, Honey, how does this find you? I am okay. I am answering Jr.'s three letters. So tell him I am answering them. How are our girls getting along? Fine I hope. Boy, I can just see those two cutting up. I just wish I could be there with all of you. I sure get lonesome to be there.

How are you these days? You be sure and take care of yourself. Darling, in answer to your comment of my love for you. You will always be my darling no matter how old you get. So I wouldn't want you to worry about looking older will bother me, as I will love you just the same. Everyone must get old. That's how the world works.

Say hello to the folks for me. Keep writing and I will do the same as I love getting your letters. No, I don't have trouble reading them at all. Tell me all about yourself. What you are doing, what the children are doing, what you are wearing? What do you dream about?

I say so long, I love you dearly. God bless you and our children. Good night and Sweet Deams.

From One Who Loves You Dearly, Charles XOXO

Dearest Darling,

Just a few lines to let you know all is okay. I hope this finds you the same. I haven't heard from you for a couple of days now, but I guess that is to be expected.

This is my day off and I know of no better way to spend it than writing to you. How do your stoves work? Do they work good or not? Has Dad and them got their fall work lined up? I'll bet you got all their fall plowing done, didn't you? Haha. What did Mom and Dad Gregory have to say in their letters? Did they get my letter yet? They should have.

Honey I hope you haven't forgotten tonight is our wedding anniversary. If I remember right, we were married September 10th or 12th. Have you?

Well, Honey all is okay here and I don't have much to write about, so I will close for now and hope to hear from you soon. Tell the children I said hello to each of them. I love you dearly and best of luck.

Your husband Charles

(author's note: They were married November 9, 1942.)

Dearest Darling,

Just a few lines to say hello and let you know I am okay.

Have you and the folks got the soy beans combined yet? Does chaff get down your neck? It used to mine. You need to watch yourself around that machinery. I wish I could be there to help you folks. Maybe if I were there we couldn't all get along together. Could we?

Well, Honey, I sure am fed up with evil but I still got some time to spend here yet. Sometimes I feel as though I might as well be dead. How is your money holding out? Do you have enough? How about that bank money? Is that gone or do you still have it?

Well, Honey, I will close saying I love you dearly. Thank you for the card and pictures.

God bless you, Charles

To the Swellest Girl I Know, My Darling Wife,

Well, I will answer the two letters I got today. I sure am glad things are working out as good as they have. I am glad the children took up with the folks like they did. I sure hope Louise and Jr. get along good in school. Honey, help Jr. study at night as it will help him later on in life. Okay? If you pack their lunches, be sure to make good lunches for them.

Honey, you can write to me here again until I stop you again. Things are so balled up here now. I don't know for nothing. I hope you and Mom don't overdo yourselves on that wallpaper hanging. You tell Alice to keep writing letters and long ones too or I will whip her when I get home.

Honey, you don't want me home with you anymore than I want to be home with you. I can imagine what feelings you have. But, what about me? You know I have those same feelings as well.

You can't tell me it was easy to bring the children to Ohio on the train. I'll bet you were about wore out when you got there. I'll bet your folks are mad as hornets at me, but it couldn't be helped.

Honey, I ain't heard from your folks lately, but they just told me the usual news and keep asking about you and wanting you to come down to Tennessee so they can see you and the children. I suppose they do worry about you all.

I heard from Sis, but she didn't have much to say. She seems to think a lot of you. She said, "Wes, Cora thinks the world of you and loves you very much." Now, she didn't tell me something I didn't already know. But I am glad you do and I love you too.

Well, I think I have answer all your questions and news is scarce over here, so I guess I had better close. So don't work too hard and take care of yourself and don't do heavy work. I mean that. Tell the children I said hello and that I love them very much.

So, Darling, I say Good Night and God bless you.,

Your husband, Charles

Dearest Darling,

Well, Honey I got your letters of November 3rd, 13th and 14th. Now Honey, if you are writing me everyday, I have to wonder where the other letters are. Maybe they got lost. Anyway the ones I do get are lots of help, so keep them coming.

I ain't been able to get Mrs. Poole address yet, but will so you can write her again. Although I don't know why you want to though. You can do as you want over Christmas, but be careful is all I ask.

Boy have I got a cold. Too much damp weather I imagine.

How are the children these days? I sure do get lonesome for them and you too.

It is about eleven o'clock. Thursday night, which is about five o'clock your time. You are probably getting ready for supper. I wish I were there to help you eat it.

Well Sweetheart I am getting sleepy and I don't feel so well, so I will close. I hope to hear from you tomorrow.

Love and best wishes, from one who loves you dearly. Say hello to everyone for me. Tell the children I love them and for them to be good for me.

Love and God Bless You,
Your husband, Charles

Dearest Darling,

Just a few lines to say hello and everything is as usual and okay. I received your letter of November 1st. It sure took a long time to get here. But I was glad to hear from you even if it was late. I really do miss it when I don't hear from you. I hadn't heard from you for two weeks.

I am sorry you are staying by yourself now. You really should have someone there with you? How are the children coming along? Are they all right? How is Roy? Has he wrote you? He should if he ain't.

Honey, about that Christmas present. I can't think of anything I need more than your letters. If I can get more mail from you is all I ask. You get yourself and the children some presents, as I can't get anything over here that is of any account.

About that calf Honey, do as you like. But don't worry about it if it is a bull. If it is a heifer, it would be a good idea to raise it. But Honey, don't go piling hard work on yourself, calf or no calf. Just do as you will, because I know you will do what is best. However it comes out is okay with me.

So I will close saying I love you dearly. God bless you. Answer soon.

Your husband, Charles

Dearest Darling,

Well, just a few lines to let you know I am well and okay. Everything here is as usual. How are you getting along now? Fine I hope. I sure am tired tonight. I ain't got no mail from you of any kind lately. I hope you haven't forgotten I am your old man and love to get letters, especially from you.

I sure am lonesome for you and miss you and the children very much. Won't I be a problem when this war is over.

How is your weather coming? Has it snowed yet? How are you getting your coal? Are you having trouble getting any? How are the children coming along Is Dad going to move or not? Did you go home for Christmas?

Honey, please write me as your letters are the only thing I look forward to. I sure do miss it when I don't get any.

Well, I will close saying I love you more than anything else in this world. God bless you and our children. Give them each a kiss for me. Love and best wishes. Answer soon

Your husband, Charles

Dearest Darling,

Well, Honey, just a few lines to let you know I am okay and hope you are a million times better than that.

I am glad you are getting along as you say in your mail. How are our children these days? Does Jr. like his new puppy? I bet you like having the puppy around some yourself.

I sure am lonesome for you tonight. I would like to be home. That is all I think about. Being home and getting loved again. I sure will never go away from you again. They would have to drag me away with a log chain. You will think I am your shadow. I think of the fun we had together many times since I've been over here. It sure is nice to have those times to look back on. It made me feel like living through them again. I often do in my dreams. And I know I will be the happiest when I am back with you and our children again.

I pray to our Father in Heaven for His kindness in any way.

God Bless You, My Darling,

Your husband, Charles XOXOX I love you.

Dearest Darling Wife,

Well, Honey, how does these few lines find you? I sure hope okay. I didn't receive any letters from you today. Maybe tomorrow I hope. I sure do look forward to your letters. If I did not have them to look forward to, I believe I would go crazy.

How are the children? Are they all well? How is Jr. doing in school? Do you think he will pass? What kind of grades does he make?

Honey, in one of your letters you said you had not heard from me in a week. Now that is something I can't help. I sure don't go a week without writing you and I don't want you to either. The mail will get there when it can, I write you very often.

How are the folks? Tell them hello for me and I will close saying I love you more than anything in this world. So God bless you my darling. Give the children my love.

Love & Kisses. Answer soon.

Your husband, Charles

Dearest Darling,

Well, Honey, just a few lines to let you know I am well and thinking of you. I started this last night but will finish it today. We have a pretty easy supper to get ready so I thought I had better finish the letter I started last night this morning, while I got the chance.

Boy, Honey, I sure do miss you and get so lonely it is all I can do not to bawl. It sure is going to be a happy day when I can come home to stay with you. Honey, I figure that with all the times I write you, you should be getting a letter everyday. Do you? Or do you get them in bunches like I do? I have got thirteen of them at once, one time.

Well, Honey, I can't think of much to write about so I will close at this time, saying I love you dearly. Give them each a kiss for me. Write and tell me all the news and all about yourself. What you are doing from one day to the next. Do you still go to church?

From one who loves you very much. More than anything in this world,

Charles

Dearest Darling Wife,

Well how do these few lines find you? Well I hope. Things are as usual here, no news of any kind.

I got a letter today that you wrote on January 3rd. It was a long time coming. Honey, you never did say what you named your dog. If you haven't named him yet why not name him Charlie. Haha What kind of dog is he?

I got a letter from Sis. She said everything was okay there. She said I may be an uncle in a week or so. I sure hope she comes through okay.

Honey, I just got done working and it just about knocked me out. I wonder what I will do when I really have to work again. How are the folks doing? Does the weather still get cold or not?

Well, Darling, I must close at this time and go to bed. God bless you and our children. From one who loves you very dearly. Tell the folks to write to me. How are the children? All well I hope.

Your husband, Charles XOXO

Dearest Darling,

Well, Honey, just a few lines to let you know I am okay. Things are as usual. No news of any kind that would be interesting to you.

I haven't sent that slip to you yet, but I will. I'll bet you were glad to get that paycheck weren't you? How are the children doing these days? Are they doing alright? How is your cow doing? Did you name her yet and if so what is it? Is she fresh? Or do you have to milk it all out of her?

Well, Honey, I sure would like to be there taking charge of things for you. I would probably have to learn all over again. But you could teach me couldn't you?

I am smoking that tobacco you sent me in a pipe. Honey, don't forget to send me those pictures of you and the children when you can. Don't forget now.

Well, I'll close for now. Out of room. God bless you and keep you safe for me. I love you dearly.

From your husband, Charles answer soon

Dearest Darling & Wife,

Well, I received four letters from you today and one from Skeet or Sis. I call her that sometimes. I sure was glad to get them and know that you were alright and well. I am okay and well. I was sure glad to get them even though they were written on January 23rd and got to me on March 15th.

Say, I thought you had gotten a battery for your radio some time ago. I read in one of your letters where you said they had one for you in Oakwood. What is it? Are you getting an extra one?

Well, what do you know! I just got four more v-mails from you just now. The latest was written January 24th. Sure am glad your cow has come fresh for you. I sure will be glad when I can be there to look after things for you like I ought to be doing. But I guess I can't help that much.

Honey, I don't know why you haven't been getting my letters. I write plenty of them. I am glad you heard from my brother Jim. Did he say where he was or not?

Boy, I get lonely for you. I get to writing you and then I get to daydreaming and thinking about the fun we use to have. Then I forget my writing and wonder why it takes me so long to write a letter. Haha.

Well, Honey I can't say much. I got the tobacco you sent me and the soap you sent also. I was glad to get it. Yes, Honey, if I need anything, I will let you know. You can be sure of that and you needn't worry about my not being able in reading your letters. Your writing is as good as mine and I really don't have trouble reading them at all. Only trouble is I don't get enough of them.

Well, Darling, I guess I had better close for now. I ain't very newsy at this time. I will write more in the morning. I love you dearly, so good night and God bless you. Take good care of you and the children for me.

Your husband, Charles Answer soon

Dearest Darling,

Well, Honey, how does this find you? Fine and dandy I hope. It leaves me okay and well but lovelorn for you. That is natural for us I guess. How are the children these days? Are they well? I hope they are.

Honey, I received seven letters from you yesterday. Was I ever glad to get them by then and know you are okay. I thought you took your cow back until she became fresh again and then you were going to take her back with you again. I guess I misunderstood that part of your letter. Can't you get milk from the folks or do you? You should be able to or don't you use milk?

Well, Honey, I guess I've asked you about enough questions at this time so I will close as everything is as usual here. So write me a long letter about you and the children. Tell me how you are getting along and everything else going on in your life. Then I can have a picture in my mind of how things are.

So, God bless you and keep you until we meet again. Give each of the children a kiss for me. Tell them I love them and you very dearly. I wrote you in several of my letters asking for pictures of you and the children. Do you think you could send me some please?

From one who loves you, Charles XOXO

Dearest Darling Wife,

Just a few lines to let you know I am fine and glad you are the same. Only, I am loving you more than ever. I just cleaned up and shaved and I sure wish I could see you now.

Honey, how is everything going by you and the children? Is everyone treating you alright? Is anyone giving you any trouble? How is your cow? Is she good? I'll bet you have a time with her. Does she ever kick you instead of the calf. Haha. How is your dog? Is he growing any? What is he? A hound, or a terrier or what?

My mail has been slow these days but I guess I'll get it when it gets here. I sure miss it when it is a long time coming.

Well, Darling, I guess I'll cut it off for now. God bless you and take care of yourself. Give my love to the children. Tell your folks hello for me and I wish them good luck.

I love you,

Your husband, Charles XOXO

Dearest Wife & Family,

Well, Honey, just a few lines to let you know I am okay. I hope this finds you the same but better. I didn't get no letter today, maybe tomorrow, I hope. Honey how are the children? All well, I hope.

Honey, did you get those pictures made or not? Are you going to have them made? I would like to have some of you. How about it?

Do you like the place where you are living now or not? Would you like to live in a better place? I just wonder if you are satisfied. Would you like to try some other place?

Please write and tell me all about yourself. How you are coming along and everything.

Well, I ain't newsy right now so I will stop asking questions and sign off for now. God bless you and keep you well and safe for me. Tell everyone I said hello to them. I love you more than anything else in the world.

Charles XOXO Answer soon.

Dearest Darling,

Well, Honey, it is Sunday night and I will answer your letter I got today. I was glad to know you are well and coming along.

What did Mom Gregory say in her letter? You know, Honey, outside of you and the folks and Skeet, I don't hear from any of the folks back there. But, you know, as long as I get your letters is all I care for. I am glad the others are okay.

Darling, you keep writing to me and I will try to write right back. Sometimes I wonder why my wife don't write to me and then I get them all at once. Then I am glad and can't complain. I don't get a letter for each day but then I reckon you don't either. But we can't complain about that either.

Someday we won't have to write letters to each other. What a happy day that will be for you and me, won't it?

Give my love to our children and God bless you and them. May he keep you all well and safe for me.

Love & Kisses, Charles

Dearest Wife & Family,

Well, Honey, just a few lines to let you know I am well and okay.

I received your box and I really do appreciate you sending it to me. But I really don't need it now as we get everything we need right now. If I really ever do need anything you can bet you will hear about it. So don't send me anything unless it is tobacco, as it will pile up on me. Candy is okay anytime, too. Oh yes! There is one thing I really do need and that is a picture taken of you and the children together.

Boy Honey, I really am looking for a letter from you tonight or tomorrow, so please write me one. How are the folks? Are they all well? How did Jr. come out with his cold? I hope he got over it okay?

Well, Honey, I will close. I'll say God bless you and our children and keep them all well for me.

Love & Kisses, Charles

February 24, 1945

Dearest Darling,

Well Honey, how does this find you? It leaves me okay. How are the children coming along? How are you coming along? Are you okay and are you satisfied or not?

How are your chickens holding up? Are your cows giving you plenty of milk? Does Jr. help with the milking? He is old enough and you will want him to help you with the chores. Tell him I want him to jump in and help his mother all he can. She has done a lot for him and I want him to show his appreciation. When I get home you can bet I will do everything I can do to make his mother's life easier.

Honey, it sure is okay by me if you give Jr. the calf money. Just let me know how much you get for the calf when you sell it. I am glad you are putting the rest of the money away as you might have use for it later on. Well, Honey, I had better close for now, so write soon. Tell everyone I said hello.

From one who loves you dearly, Charles

Dearest Wife,

Well, just a few lines to let you know I am okay. I received a letter today addressed to me from Camp Gruber. Honey, all those letters addressed to Camp Gruber are catching up with me now. That is why I wasn't receiving any letters from you when I first got here. I am glad to get them even if they are late. I began to think you had gotten tired of me or that you were mad because I brought you to Ohio.

You said in one of your letters that you will be glad when this war is over so I can come home. Honey, you will never know how glad I will be when I do get to come home to you and the children as well as my folks. It sounds as if they really need me on their farm and that may be where our future lies. Anyway that will be a great day for me. We won't be the only happy people. Other boys and their families will be just as happy, too. We will all be one happy bunch when that time comes.

This weather does not seem to agree with my sinuses. I am having trouble with them again.

Honey, how are the children these days? I hope you have plenty of warm clothes for them. Be sure to take good care of them as well as yourself for me. Have you got your cow yet? I hope so. If so, does she give good milk? I reckon you will get fat drinking milk. I hope so anyway.

Well, Honey, I can't think of much else to write so I will close. Hope to hear from you real often.

God bless you,

Your husband, Charles

Dearest Wife,

Just a few lines to say I am okay. I am getting your letters as well as can be, I guess. I am glad you enjoyed your brother Roy's visit. Sure wish I could have been there to see him. Mom and Dad wrote me telling me they were there for dinner and you and Roy danced for them. I am glad you all enjoyed yourselves. I knew a girl who never seemed to like to dance with a certain party when the notion struck. But, Honey, anything is good that breaks the monotony, isn't it?

Dad said they might move. Maybe. This is the first I've heard of it. I hope it is for the better and not the worse. I hope Sis gets better before her next increase. Who is staying with you now? No one I guess.

How is everything going by you now? How is your cow? Is she getting milk? The folks say Earl got married. Do you know anything about it? How are the children doing in school? Does Louise like school or not?

Well, I can't think of much to say for now. It is 10 o'clock in the evening here and about three o'clock in the morning there. So I guess you are snoring away. I am glad you got your stove and radio. I am sure you enjoy it. I ain't listen to a radio since I left America. They are scarce over here.

Well, Honey, I will close saying I miss you.

God bless you and the children, Charles

Dearest Darling,

Well, just a few lines to say hello and to ask how you are. How is everyone there? Have you been missing my mail? I ain't got no mail for two weeks now.

How are the children? Are you all keeping warm? What about that farm Mom & Dad bought? What do you think of it? Have you heard from your mom and day lately? Boy, I haven't heard from anyone. Boy, Sweetheart, I sure do miss your letters. I keep looking for them everyday. I think they will come once the Christmas rush is over.

Well, I can't think of anything to write. Just questions and they ain't interesting to read. So I will close, saying I love you. Answer soon and kiss the children for me and give them my love.

God bless you, be good and take care,

Your husband, Charles

Dearest Darling,

Just a few lines to answer your five letters that I got yesterday. Boy was I glad to get them. Everything here is as usual.

I got a Christmas box from that church you are going to. It had some soap in it and boy I really needed it. Soap is scarce over here.

We really enjoy the cake and candy, too. When anyone gets a box over here, it doesn't last very long because everyone helps himself as though it was sent to them, too. Just one big happy family. Haha. When you go to church, thank them for me and tell them it was in good shape. Also, that the boys enjoyed it as well as myself.

Honey, I am glad you and Dad are getting along well. He is a good guy if you stay on the right side of him.

Darling, I must close saying I love you dearly.

From your old man, Charles

Dearest Wife,

Well a few lines to let you know that I am okay and so is everything else, I guess. How is everything there? How are the children coming along? How does your radio work?

Well this is Sunday. Sure would like to be at home. What are you doing these days and how are you doing? Do you go to church anymore? Do the kids? Do you hear anything from the folks in Tennessee? What do they have to say?

How are you doing? Are you alright? How are the folks doing? Are the folks planning on moving and if so what about you? How are Jr. and Louise coming along in school? Does she like it or not? Do they get good grades? I hope so. How is Betty? Is she still a chatterbox? Tell her that her daddy says she is full of prunes. Haha.

Well, Honey, I sure do miss you. I never knew I could miss a wife so bad, but one never knows, does he? I'll sure know when I get back how much my wife and kids mean to me. It sure takes a lot to wake someone up, but my eyes are wide open now. You never said how your stove works, yet.

Well, I can't think of much to write as I haven't heard from you for two weeks. I hope you are still writing. I write to you everyday and sometimes twice. Tell me all about how you and the children are getting along and what you are doing. I am homesick and don't mind admitting it. I have been for a week and a nice long letter would help me out. So how about it?

Everything is the same day after day. We get a lot of colds here. Something is wrong about the weather here.

Honey, I will close for now. God bless you and good luck.

Your husband, Charles

Dearest Darling Wife & Family,

Just a few lines to let you know I am okay and well. Hope this finds you the same.

Honey, I got a letter from Burt and Evelyn. They are okay and doing good according to their letter. Boy, I sure wish I was as lucky as they are. Out of the army and have a baby already. He sure didn't lose any time. I wonder if his leg still bothers him. Maybe I'll develop a bad leg. Haha

I wrote to your Mom and pop today. How are you and my folks getting along? As good as can be expected, I reckon. How are you all doing?

Well, there isn't enough news to write about of any kind, so I will close for now. I've got to go wash and shave as I have duty at noon. So, Darling, be good and be sure to write and tell the folks I am okay.

May God bless you and the children. Say hello to all.

From your husband, Charles XOXO

Dearest Darling,

Well, Honey, just a few lines to let you know I am okay. Only very lonesome for you. Boy, I miss you. I have dreamt of you for the last two nights. I thought I was home for Christmas dinner and we sure was having a swell time. I sure wish it had been true. I was beginning to think I have no love but your letters tell me different.

Honey, how are the children? Are they okay? Hope none of them are sick. How are you?

You know Honey, I don't get much mail from you but I sure enjoy what I get. I know of one wife who is going to get a good spanking for not writing more when I get home. Do you know who I mean? Everyone else gets their wives letters so I can't understand the reason for not getting mine. So, one day you had better have a real good reason.

So, Honey, I will close hoping this finds you all well. God bless keep you and keep you.

Your husband, Charles

Dearest Darling,

Just a few lines to say hello and that everything is okay. I hope this finds you the same and better. I miss you. Well, Honey, today is

Armistice Day. Wouldn't it be great if history could just repeat itself and we could avoid this war. Boy oh boy!!

I am off duty until Monday. Sure wish I could be home. There isn't anyplace around here for a fellow to spend his time, so there is no sense leaving. I read most of the time. You know I got eight letters from you the other day. Most of them were from Camp Gruber and not sent directly to me over here. I sure was glad to get them anyway.

I guess I will close for now as there ain't much to say. Everything is about the same day after day. So, I'll say God bless you. Be good and careful.

Your husband, Charles

P.S. The only thing good about this war is that it is the only reason we met. If only we could be together.

Dearest Darling,

Just a few lines to let you know I am okay. I ain't heard from you for a couple of days, but the worst part of it is that I ain't got those pictures yet. Are you having trouble getting them made? I bet you are or I would have had them. I hope you don't mind me growling about it. You can just imagine a how anxious I am to get them. The ones I have are all faded and worn. Be sure to send me one of you and the children taken together.

How are the children these days? All well, I hope. I am sure glad you have them. I sure would like to see you all again. That would mean so much to me. how are you getting along these days? Do you have enough money or do you need more. How are people treating you back there? How are you and the Wistner's getting along? Are you still going to church?

Well, Sweetheart, I don't know much to write about, so I will close saying God bless you and keep you and the children safe for me.

From one who loves you dearly,
Your husband, Charles

P.S. Tell everyone hello for me. Love& Kisses I Love you

Dearest Darling,

Just a few lines before I go to bed to let you know I am okay and hope you are the same.

How are our children? Are they well? How are they coming along in school? How is your weather now? Is it cold or hot? Honey, I didn't get any mail today. Maybe tomorrow. Do you think I will get any? How are Mom and Dad these days?

Honey, do you still go to church or not? Do you go to town? How did you make out with that suit of mine. Did you get it cut down for Jr.? Did you do it? Or what? Let me know how it looked if you did.

Well, Darling, news is scarce and I ain't very windy tonight. I guess I had better sign off and go to bed. So I'll say good night and God bless you and the children and keep you all well and safe for me.

From one who loves you more than anything else in this world,

Your old man, Charles I Love You

Dearest Darling,

I will answer the two letters I got from you last night. Was really glad to get them. Was also glad to know you are alright and Jr. got over his cold okay.

I was just kidding about naming the dog after me. I think the name you gave him is a fine one.

The days we spent together were the happiest I ever had in my life, too and I'm sure counting on spending more together with you when this war is over. I was sure happy when we were together. I think we did just fine together, considering everything. Not many people thought we would get along as well as we do. Don't you think we do?

You said you sold a can of milk. That old cow of yours must give lots of milk. How much do you get for a can of milk? Honey, isn't Jr. big enough to do the milking for you or do you not think so? I believe he could if you would learn him. I wish I was there so I could do it for you. I would like that.

I had better sign off and go to bed. So good night and God bless you.

From one who loves you more dearly than anything else in this world,

Your husband, Charles

Love & Kisses

January, 9, 1945

Dear Son,

Well, Boy, I received your letter and sure was glad to hear from you.

Yes, Jr. I noticed the downhill lines but that is nothing. I write downhill all the time. You just keep on trying and you will get over that.

How is our Mama getting along these days? Hope you are taking good care of her like I asked you to. Is she getting out in the cold? Do you get her coal and wood in for her at night so she does not have to get out in the cold to get it?

How are Betty and Louise getting along? Make them be careful and not get sick.

Now do you like it where you are now? Do you like Kenny and Danny? Do they give you a hard time?

Well Son, be sure to keep writing to me. So God bless you all.

Your Daddy, Charles Hugs & Kisses to you all.

Dearest Darling,

Well, Honey just a few lines to let you know I am okay.

This is Sunday and I am working or suppose to be. But I got to take time to write my honey a few lines. I am thinking of you so much today that my heart ache with loneliness. So if I get into trouble it will be worth it. What can they do? Throw me out of the army and send me back home? If only it was that easy. I am kidding. They need me here or at least they say they do. So I will stay willingly but not gladly.

You say you think I don't love you as much as I did. It is only you that I want. Say you don't want to be my wife anymore? Just say so, because I won't let you go anyhow.

Are your potatoes growing any? How will you store them? Will you have wood cut for the winter? Now don't go cutting it yourself. You have Dad or Danny do it for you. How are the folks anyway? Are they doing well? Have you seen or heard from my sis, lately? How are Alice and Danny doing?

Well Darling, I will close saying I love you and our children dearly from the very bottom of my heart. Sending you all my love.

Your husband, Charles SWAK

Dearest Wife,

Just a few lines to let you know I am well and okay. I got your letter last night and was glad to know you are okay too.

Honey, I got a good cold in my head today. I don't think my body will ever get used to the weather here in England. Let me know when you buy your bathing suit. About those pictures you were going to take and send me. Have you taken them yet? I am waiting not so patiently for them by now.

Life is gloomy these days. I bet you are keeping busy, ain't you? How are the children these days? Are they well? Are they going to school?

Well Honey, as usual, there ain't no news of any kind. How are the folks these days? Are they well? Tell them to write and you do the same. Okay?

So I will close saying God bless you and keep you for me.

From one who loves you dearly, Charles Love &m Kisses

Dearest Darling,

Just a few lines to answer your letter which I received today. I am glad you are getting along okay. Everything over here is the same, no news of any kind. Just the same old routine day after day.

Now Honey, about that bedroom suite. You know it is okay by me. In fact, I am for it. Be sure to get a good one and don't let anyone stiff you on it. Take someone along who understands that stuff. But above all, get one that you like and not one that someone has talked you into buying. Darling, you don't need to worry about me not wanting you to purchase one because it will be okay by me. You go right ahead and get what you want to.

Well Honey, my speaker is going off for dinner so I will close. God bless you and keep you all safe for me until I come home again. Tell everyone I said hello and to write to me often.

From one who loves you dearly,

Your husband, Charles XOXO SWAK

Dearest Wife & Family,

Well Honey, a few lines to answer the letter that I haven't got yet. So I'll answer it anyway. I am fine and okay. Hope this finds you well and better. How are the children? All well I hope.

This is Sunday night and I sure would like to be home. This war sure is dragging on. Seems like a day is a year. I reckon it is the same for you. How are the folks coming along? Are they well?

Honey, I sure am anxious for those pictures. We had chicken for dinner today. What did you have?

Well, Darling I am running out again so I will close and sign off for now. May God bless and keep you safe and well for me. Always remember this, I love you more than anything else in this world.

Charles

Dearest Darling,

Well, Honey, just a few lines to let you know I am okay. Things are as usual, no news of any kind. I didn't receive a letter from you today. Maybe I will get one tomorrow, if not two.

How are the children? All well and growing I hope. Honey, write and tell me if you got your bedroom suite and what is it like? How are you these days? Are you doing well? How is your livestock coming along? How is the calf coming? Is he growing any? What are you going to use as pasture for the cow? Do you think there is enough pasture around the barn? Is the chicken lot out behind your house?

Honey, I love you more than you will ever know.

Charles Love & Kisses

Dearest Darling,

Honey, I just got the letter you wrote saying that you got everything straightened out at the bank. How do you mean you got things straightened out? Honey, sometimes you leave words out and it is hard for me to get the meaning of the sentence. Also put the date on each letter. I am sending all my letters so you can get them at home.

Tell me why you asked me if the fellows are out here with me. I hope the boil doesn't fester and pester you too much. By the time you have gotten this you will have forgotten all about the boil. I hope so. I have just read all of my letters over again and have disposed of them as I have no place to keep them. But I do like to read them over again though.

How is the cider? Stout, I bet. Haha

From your husband,

Dearest Darling,

Well Honey just a few lines to let you know I am okay. I hope it finds you the same. Boy, Honey, I haven't heard from you for almost four days. I hope you haven't forgotten all about me. Have you?

Honey, how are the children? Are they well or not? How is everything going by you? Alright or not? Are you able to get the things you need.

How is Sis doing? I haven't heard from her so I am supposing she has gone to the hospital to have her new increase?

Say, has your cow jumped over the moon lately? Haha. How is the calf coming along? Is he growing? I hope your cow and calf appreciate my thoughts of them. I appreciate having something to ask about. Do the children like their new home? Do they like it or not?

Well, Darling, news is scarce. God bless you and keep you safe for me.

I love you.

Your husband, Charles XOXO

Dearest Wife,

Just a few lines to let you know I am well and okay. Honey, I am going to put the bank note in this letter, so be sure and let me know when you receive it.

About the pasture for the cow, why don't you see if you could rent pasture for her in that pasture by the house. When it dries up in the summer, you could take her out around the barn lot to the road.

Honey, there ain't much I can talk about. Have you got your chickens and if so, how many? Do they lay any eggs? Are you going to have any meat for next winter? How are the folks? Are they well?

Honey, which do you think would be best for you? To buy your meat in town or to raise it on hoof and butcher it? Which would you rather do? You do just as you think for yourself. It would be lots of work though, you know.

Well, God bless you and keep you safe for me.

From one who loves you dearly,
Your husband, Charles XOXO

Dearest Darling,

Just a few lines to answer your letter I got today. Sure was glad to know you all are okay and well. Yes Honey, I wish I were there putting sugar in your coffee and stirring it up. Honey, things will be all quiet someday and the world will be back to normal. And decent people can be happy, again. We will have our happiness then.

Honey, what are you doing besides trying to stay warm now? Are the children all okay? Honey I am still looking for those pictures. I hope you got them made. The ones I have of you now are fading from carrying them around so long.

Well, Darling, I ain't so newsy right now so I will close and write more this evening. So Honey, answer real soon and may God bless and keep you safe and well for me.

Tell the folks I said hello and for them to write me occasionally.

From the one who loves you, Charles I Love You

April, 1945 (England)

Dearest Darling,

Well Honey just a few lines to let you know I am okay and well.

How are the children? All well I hope. Honey, you tell Jr. to save all his money that he can and I may borrow it off of him when I come home. Haha. I do think it is a good idea for him to learn to save money.

Honey, I don't think I can have my pictures made just now, but I will as soon as I can. Be sure and send me some pictures of you.

Right now it is Friday night and exactly nine o'clock. I pull shift tomorrow about three o'clock, your time. I suppose about the time you are thinking about what to cook for supper. Well, a nice big hamburger will always be okay for my supper. Can you cook one for me too? Like the ones you cooked for me when we were out in California together? I was so happy then. Were you?

Well Darling, I must close and go to bed. God bless you and the children and keep you all safe for me. Good night. I love you.

Charles SWAK

Dearest Wife & Family,

Well, how does this find you? All well and okay, I hope. It leaves me okay but lonesome and homesick, longing to be home with you all. How are you and the children coming along? Are they well? What are they doing now? Are they still in school or not?

Honey, how does Louise do in school? Does she seem to like to go? Were they able to get on the bus in front of the house or did they have to walk to the corner? How does Jr. like school this year? I want you to be sure and keep at him to make him want to go to school.

Well, Darling, I am getting sleepy. I have been up since four o'clock this morning and that makes for a pretty long day. Boy, I will be sure glad to see this year end. I know a lot others who do too. That will be a happy day for me.

So God bless you and keep you well and safe for me.

Your husband, Charles XOXO

Dearest Darling,

Just a few lines to let you know I am okay and thinking of you.

How are you and the children by now? Honey, when do they get out of school for summer? Or do you know yet?

I am glad you got the letter with the note in it. It may be a good idea to keep the bank note yourself. Not that I don't trust those people but just to be on the safe side. Honey, are you getting along okay? How are things going by you? Do you have too much work to do or not? You got to watch and not get too much stock that it would be hard for you to look after it.

How about the pictures? Am I going to get them? I hope so. I got a letter from Earve and Aggie. They said they were coming down to see you. I hope you all had a good time when they came. Has Uncle Harve ever come to see you?

Well, Honey, I will close and write a few lines to the folks. So may the Good Lord Bless & Keep You safe for me. I love you.

Your husband, Charles SWAK

Dearest Wife,

Well, Honey just a few lines to let you know I am okay and hope this finds you the same, well and better. How are the children? Well & better as well.

What are you doing these days? How is your weather? Is it warm now? I'll bet it is wet now. Usually, it is at this time of the year. I sure wish I was there with you all. Sometimes I don't think this war is ever going to end. It is lasting longer than I thought it would.

How are the children? Are they still going to school or is it out for the summer? How does Louise like going to school?

Well, I can't think of much more I can write about. Only more questions than a smart person can answer, I guess.

I will close, saying God bless you and the children.

Your husband, Charles XOXO

Dearest Wife & Family,

Just a few lines to let you know I am thinking of you. I hope this finds you okay and well. It leaves me okay. I just got some washing and cleaning done in general. Now, all I need is some place to go. Haha.

I haven't been getting any mail of late. But I guess that is to be expected, the way we move around and all.

How are the folks doing now? Buzzing around like bees around honey, I bet. What are you doing? Buzzing around, too, I guess. Haha.

Well, Honey, I can't think of much to say so keep the home fires burning and I will see you when this was is over with.

God bless you and keep you. From one who loves you dearly. Tell the folks I said hello.

Your husband, Charles SWAK

Dearest Wife & Family,

Well just a line to say I received your letter of the 8th and was sure glad to get it. It isn't so bad considering everything.

Well, Honey, there isn't much to say or write you, only I would like to be at home. But who doesn't? Only about a million other guys. How are you getting along now? How are the children? When does school let out?

Boy it is a job to write a letter when you don't have anything you can talk about. You can say the same thing over and over again. It gets old after so long.

So I'll say so long and God bless you,

Your husband, Charles XOXO Say hello to everyone for me.

My Dearest Darling,

Well Honey, just a few more lines to answer the letter I received tonight. I got an answer to the letter I sent to Earl while I was in England. He said "Hi" and he was okay. He is still stationed in Virginia. He sure is lucky. I envy him.

How are the children coming along this time of year? Are they still in school? Tell them I said hello to them.

Honey, you give me heck for not writing now. You should take it easy and not get excited. You shouldn't worry. I write as often as it is handy. So you take it easy and take care of the kids and I'll do the writing.

How is your garden coming along? Is it growing? I hope so.

Well say hello to the folks for me. I'll close for now.

All my Love and Kisses, Charles

My Dearest Darling,

Well just a few more lines to let you know I am okay and better. This has been a long night for me. I did a big washing yesterday and it ain't dry yet. We are going to have an inspection today and some of my clothes are going to be a wet inspection.

I got two letters from you today and boy was I glad to get them. I am sorry I can hardly think of what to write. There are times when I can hardly write anything at all. You know how that is.

How are you these days? Anyway I don't care when you go to church. I just wondered why you went at night. Sorry if I made you sore. I guess you mistook me, but that is okay. I have been mistook by lots of people, haven't you?

Well, Darling, I must stop now. May God Bless and keep you for me.

Love & Kisses Charles XOXO

Dearest Darling Wife,

Well, how does this find you? It leaves me okay. Everything here is as usual. No news of any kind except the same.

I just got done having a sponge bath. I think I'll fry up some potatoes now and call it a day. It sure has been a nice day. One of those days that make you want to be home. I get so disgusted I could just go off and die someplace. But I don't reckon that would cut the war any shorter.

How are the children? I'll bet Betty is getting to be a big girl now.

Well, I can't think of very much to write about just now, so I guess I had better sign off. You be sure to write to me often. I write as often as I can.

The people over her walk around and look as if we were freaks of nature or something. I reckon they would like to cut our necks. Some of them anyway.

Well Darling, God bless you and the children and keep you well and safe for me.

Love & Best Wishes, Charles XOX

Dearest Cora, My Wife,

Well, Honey, just a few lines to let you know I am okay. I haven't heard from you for almost a week now. I only got one letter last week and that was from Alice. She said Skeet was having a hard time. Boy, I hope she comes along okay with the baby. She said Mom was still with them. Are you cooking for Dad and the boys? Or are they keeping bachelor?

Honey I popped my first corn last night. I found two ears in the storeroom so I popped it. Boy it was good.

Darling I never have heard about those pictures you were going to send me. I hope you are going to send them to me, soon. How do you like your new bedroom suite? How are the children? All well, I hope. Tell the folks hello for me and for them to write to me. I got a letter from your Mom. She said everyone was okay there. I am glad.

Well, I will close saying God bless you and the children and keep you safe for me. I love you more dearly each day.

Your husband, Charles XXOXO

Dearest Darling & Wife,

Well Honey, just a few lines this morning to let you know I am okay and thinking of you. How is everything on the home front today? Are you all well? How are the children coming along in school?

Honey, has it stopped raining there yet? That is the nice thing about the weather there. You get a taste of all kinds. Honey, have you sent those pictures yet? I bet you are having a hard time getting them made.

Boy, I wish I could be there with you. I keep praying everyday for this war to end. But it just keeps dragging on. But there is a day coming sometime when all of this will be over.

So I will close saying God bless you and keep you and the children well and safe for me. Tell everyone I said hello to them. From one who loves you dearly,

Your husband, Charles I Love You

Dearest Darling Wife,

Well Honey, just a few lines to see how you are coming along? I am glad you were okay when you wrote them but they were all dated the middle of March.

How is Sis and her baby coming along? I'll bet she and Nelson are right proud of their new population. I know I would be. Wouldn't you?

I am glad our children are all okay. Yes I bet that Betty is a job for you all by yourself. I would like to be there to get in your way too, like I use to. If I were there, you would be mad at me most of the time. But I wouldn't mind if I was there for you to get mad at. I would give you that spanking like I always promised you.

Well, Darling, I've got some clothes boiling and I need to take a bath for a change, so I had better close. I need to write Skeet tonight also. God bless you and our children and keep you all, safe for me. From one who loves you very much. Tell all the folks hello for me and for them to write.

From your husband, Charles

Dearest Wife & Family,

Just a few lines to let you know I am okay and well. Honey be sure to use my new A.P.O. number. It is 230. How is everything going by you? You know I haven't received those pictures yet.

This is the first I've written in several days as we have been moving around quite a bit. How are the children? How are the folks? All are well I hope.

I cut my finger this morning and it is unhandy for me to write. I hope you can read this mess.

When are you going to see your folks again? It is alright by me anytime you feel like going. Just be careful when traveling.

Well, Honey, I can't think of much to say so I will close at this time and write more later. Be sure to give my folks my love and give them my new A.P.O. number.

God bless you and keep you well and safe for me. Answer soon.

From your husband, Charles XOXO

Dearest Wife,

Well, Honey, how does this find you? All well, I hope. It leaves me well but lazy as ever. Boy, I wish I was home. I really get lonesome for you. How are the children coming along? Are they well?

I can't think of much to write about, as everything is the same day after day. There isn't any news of any type I can talk about.

Honey, do ever hear from any of my brothers? If you do, what do they have to say? Has your weather gotten any warmer or not? I hope it has.

Well, I've got to shave and clean up and wash out some of my clothes. You know I have to keep them washed myself now. I can't have you do them until I come back. Don't I wish I could. Haha. Do you remember how dirty I used to get in one day? It is twice as bad here. Maybe I will get a German boy to do my wash for me. They are always asking for a job of sorts.

Well, Sweet heart, I will close. So God bless you and our children. I love you all more dearly than anything in this world.

From your husband, Charles

Tell everyone back there I said hello.

Dearest Darling,

Well, Honey, just a few lines to let you know all is okay here. How are things back there? I see by the papers we get here that it was warm there for awhile. I bet you are glad to see warm weather come. I know I would like to see summer come here. But I am still glad for your benefit. Are you sowing any oats yet? It is about time isn't it? What are Pop and the boys doing now?

Honey, about those pictures. Will I ever get them? I sure want them. Well every thing is the same over here and doesn't amount to much. I guess I will close and hope for a letter from you tonight. I guess that is a job for you as much as it is for me at times.

Tell all I said hello and God bless you and the children and keep you safe and well for me. From one who loves you dearly,

Your husband, Charles

Dearest Darling,

Just a few lines to let you know that I am well and okay. I hope this finds you the same except a million times more.

How are the children? Okay and well? How are the folks coming along? Are they doing any spring planting? How is Skeet coming along? Is she getting along after the birth?

Honey, nothing much has happened that I can write about just now. I got your letter you wrote to me March 7th. That is not too bad. Haha.

Yes Darling, I will be glad when I can be at home and I sure hope I t won't be too long. I am sure fed up over here. But what can I do?

I haven't received any pictures yet and you haven't said anything in your letters about them. Have you had them taken or not.?

Well, Darling, I had better close for now. God bless you and keep you well and safe for me. I love you dearly.

Your husband, Charles XOXO

Dearest Darling Wife,

Well, Honey, just a few lines to let you know I am well and okay.

I got a letter from Harve and Mary the other day. They had been down to Mom & Pop's place. I guess they didn't stay long.

Honey, how are you and the Miller's coming along? Do any of them come to see you these days? Do you still go to church on Sundays? Have you seen anything of Harve and Mary Harshman lately? Or do they come our? How did Harve's leg come out? Does he still walk with a cane?

Honey, Have you heard from your folks or haven't you written them lately? How do the folks seem to be coming along on the farm? Do they have their corn planted yet? Do you drive their tractor any? Now tell me the truth. Do you or don't you?

Honey, I can't think of much more to accuse you of so I will close for now. So be good and God bless you and keep you safe and well for me.

All My Love,
Your husband, Charles

Answer soon. Be sure and use my new address. Tell all I said hello. Honey, try writing me some air mail. I believe it will come just as fast as V-Mail if not faster now. God bless you, my Darling, Charles

Dearest Darling,

Just a few lines to let you know I am okay and to answer your letter that I received today. I am glad you are all okay. Everything here is the same. Nothing new to speak of.

Well, Honey, I hope you can get those pictures taken soon. My cold is better now and I have forgotten about it. It only lasted two days. I used some Vicks and it didn't take long to kick it.

I am glad you got pictures taken of your cow. Send some along with the other pictures of you and the children.

Well, Darling, I am looking forward to that picture of your cow. I just might tell the boys here that it is you. Haha. Just kidding, but please send the pictures of you. I will pin it on the wall along with the picture of your cow so they will know the difference. Again, I kid. To me you are the most beautiful girl in the world and I want to show you off. I also need to see how everyone has changed.

From the one who loves you dearly and longs for you constantly.

Your husband, Charles XOXO

Dearest Wife,

Well, a few lines to let you know I am okay and well. I hope this finds you the same and better. How are the children? All well I hope.

I just got done doing about a month's washing and you know how I hate to wash. Have you got any garden in yet?

Boy, the kids have grown according to the pictures. I haven't seen any change in you except for the better. I look at the pictures everyday. I sure am proud of them. I showed them to all the boys here and they say I have a fine looking family. You look very good in them.

Well, Honey, I go on duty in the kitchen in one half hour. So I had better close. Everything here is as usual and I can't think of much more to write.

So good luck and God bless you all.

From your husband, Charles XOXO

Dearest Darling,

Well Honey, just a few lines to let you know I am okay and thinking of you. Sure is a nice day here. It rained last night and it cooled down a bit.

I got me a new pair of overalls. I have three pair now so that means I won't have to wash as much. I think I will have some of my laundry done by the Germans. As I don't seem to like doing it myself, as you know. Haha

I would like to see that new suite you bought. Is it a good one? Where did you buy it? I hope you are paying cash and not going into debt or anything. Or have you?

How are the folks doing? Have they harvested any grain yet? Honey, I sure hope your chickens are doing good because I like fried chicken. Haha. But they will be too old to fry by the time I get there.

Well dear, I can't think of any news as there isn't any. Saying I love you shouldn't be news by now. You do know it, don't you? I sure hope so.

Honey, have you had any boyfriends since I've been gone. I'd better not know it if you have.

Well Baby, I will close and write you after supper. May God keep you well and safe for me.

Sending all my love,

Your husband, Charles XOXO

Dearest Darling,

Well Honey, just a few lines this evening to say hello and all is fine. I didn't get any mail from you today, but maybe I will tomorrow. I sure hope so anyway.

Boy it sure is lonesome and dreary over here. I sure do get tired of this kind of life. I just got done eating an egg sandwich and it made me think of those hamburgers you use to make me in Oklahoma. Boy, those were sure swell days and I enjoy having the memories of them. Sure would like to be back there again.

How are the folks? Are they well? What are they doing about moving? Are they or ain't they going to move?

Honey, have you gotten any letters from Roy since he was up there?

Well, Sweetheart, all I can do is ask more questions as there ain't any news over here, just the same old routine. So I say God bless you and our children. Please write often.

From your husband, Charles

Say hello to all.

Dearest Darling,

Well, Honey, just a few lines to let you know I am okay and all is well over here. Boy, I surely am a proud boy as I got nine letters from you today. So I feel a lot better now. I am going to write a long letter and answer each one of them today. So you can expect another one after this one. I also will write a few lines to the children.

Say, about that calf and cow business. Are you planning on going in to dairy business. I want you to be careful in working around with that saw or anything else you may work with. I may have to have Dad fire you if you don't. Haha. But Darling please do be real careful.

Boy, Darling I really have been worrying about you as I hadn't gotten any mail. I sure feel better now. But as it is late, I will close this letter and write more in the morning.

So I will say I love you, more than anything else in this world. Give each of our children a kiss and a hug for me.

God bless you and answer soon, I Love You, Charles

Dearest Wife & Family,

Well, honey, just a few lines to let you know I am well and okay. Everything here is as usual. How are you getting along now? Fine I hope.

Boy, Honey, I received about nine letters from you in the last two days. I am going to answer your letter on this kind of paper so you can get it quicker. I would get yours quicker if you would write it v-mail but you write anyway you want to, just as long as you write.

Now, about those pants. You do as you want. If Dad wants them and you want him to have them then it is alright by me.

Honey, I know you are getting along good but I sure do miss you. If I even get out of the army, I won't know how to act. I will be so happy. How are the children? Tell them I love them very much too.

Well, Honey, I had better sign off as I am getting very sleepy, as usual. Do you remember how sleepy I use to get? Haha. I can.

Bye now, Charles

Dearest Darling,

Well Honey I will answer the two letters I just got,

I am glad you had good luck with your chickens. Boy, I can just taste the fried chicken now. Oh Boy! Yes Honey, I received the popcorn you sent me. I popped it and ate until I about busted. Haha.

There isn't very much news here. Everyone is wondering what Japan is going to do. I sure hope she gives up soon. Boy, I sure get disgusted over here. Good times wasted and lives are passing on and I am just doodling away my time. The army sure got the best five years of my life and lots of other guys too.

How is everything there? Honey, I would very much like to have my dinner. Can I have it or not. Are you saving it for me?

Well, I can't think of much more to say. May God bless you and keep you safe and well for me. I love you.

Your husband, Charles

Dearest Wife & Family,

Well, Dear, I reckon by the time you get this you will be hot around the collar. Everything here is as good as can be expected. I am in Germany and have been for some time. I didn't say so in my letters. I guess you could tell. I couldn't say much at all.

I received more of your pictures. They were nice. One of the children faces wee blurred, though. I just had some fried potatoes. We are living in a house in a town.

I'm glad you are going to church. Why do you go at night? Do you walk or do people carry you? I sure don't like you living alone like that. Can't you get someone to live with you?

I'm glad you sold your cow. How are the folks coming along on the farm?

Well, Honey, I can't think of much more to say. So God bless you and the children.

Your husband, Charles XOXO

Dearest Wife & Family,

Well Darling, how are these days finding you? It leaves me okay.

Well, Honey, I guess it is okay to tell you where we are now. I am about forty miles from the border of Germany in a small burg named Austnaluft (?). So if you can find that on the map you will have a faint idea of where I am. I can think of other places I would rather be.

How are our children these days? Are they all well and growing I bet. How often do you get to town these days? Do the folks go very often?

I reckon you are all busy now. That old cow of yours must have been a pretty good one to bring that kind of price.

Well, I've got some work to do so I'd better get busy on it. God bless the children and keep you all safe for me.

With all my love and best of everything to you. Answer soon.

Your husband, Charles XOXO

Germany, May 14, 1945

Dearest Wife,

Well, just a few lines to let you know I am well and good. I have started to work the night shift now, but I don't know how long it will last though.

We sure are having nice weather now. I hope you are too. I got your letter of April 22nd today and sure was glad to hear from you. Honey, you should have been getting my letters as I have been writing pretty regular the last week or so.

We are having creamed chicken tomorrow. We are getting it ready tonight.

What is the news there or is there any? Are your potatoes growing that you planted? How are the children? Who is bigger? Louise or Betty? I'll bet they are growing.

Boy, I sure will be glad when I can be there to see you again. Time sure goes slow for me anymore. I sure hope I don't have to stay in the army as long as I have already. Sure seems like a long time. I can't see how we could be at war as long as we have already been by now. I sure hope Japan can be whipped soon.

Well, Darling I must close for now. Kiss and hug the children for me. Someday we may be together again. I pray that we are.

God bless you all,
Your husband, Charles

Germany.
May 15, 1945

Dearest Wife,

I will write you a few lines to let you know I am fine and better. I hope this finds you the same and better.

Honey, I've got to have the children's birth date and age so please send it to me. I did have it on a card but I can't find the card now. So send it to me with their full age and birth date. Now don't forget. I've got to turn it in at headquarters.

Everything over here is okay. We sure are having some nice weather and hope you are too. How is everything going by you? Fine I hope. Are you working hard these days? We are going to get some down training I guess.

Well, honey, I see by the newspapers that a lot of boys are getting out of the army. They sure are lucky guys. I only wish I was one of them. I can't think of anything I would like better than to be out of here and be home. But I guess I wasn't born lucky at times like these.

Have you heard from your folks lately? I haven't heard from anyone as we haven't been getting our mail regularly, as of late. But it will straighten out soon. How are the folks doing? Have they got any corn planted yet?

Has the weather been wet this spring. People over here use all oxen for farming. It is slow to watch them but they seem to get the work done. They farm in strips. I suppose to keep away erosion, mostly.

Well. Honey, don't, don't waste any time sending the children's full name, age and birth dates, so I can turn them in.

So for now, good luck and God bless you and the children and keep you safe for me.

Your husband, Charles All my love and kisses. Tell all I said hello. Take care of yourself.

May 26, 1945

Well just a few lines to let you know I am okay. Sure hope this finds you the same. Or better.

This makes three letters I've written in the last twelve hours. It is really a good past time, especially since I have the time to pass. I've been thinking of you all day and night. I am in one of my lonely moods now and I reckon you are glad as you get more mail again that way.

I have got my work done for the night and my feet are sure tired although I haven't done all that much. You say you go to church almost every night. I am glad you can go as it will help you pass the time. I sure would like to be there to go along. Do you think you could get me to go to church with you? What do you do during the daytime? Do you still have your chicks? Are they growing? Do you still have that dog? Are you making garden?

Well, Honey, I can't think of very much else to write about. You can try to answer all my questions you can. I reckon you have a big job on your hands.

Do you ever hear anything of your ex or not? What are Mom & Dad doing now? Why are they fixing up that house for on that place they bought. Is someone going to live in it?

I want you to write me an air-mail letter and tell me everything you think to tell me. Whether you think it is any of any interest or not.

I've written and asked several people, including you. Who did Jim marry? But I guess you all don't think it is my business to know.

Well, Honey, I had better close as I am getting sleepy and the longer I write the sleepier I get. You know how I am when I get sleepy.

So for now, Honey, I will say so long and God bless you. Tell everyone back there I said hello and give them my best wishes and they should drop me a line every now and then. I know they are busy but a few lines is better than none at all.

I will ring off now, sending you all my love. From one who loves you dearly,

Your Husband, Charles.

Dearest Wife,

Well, Honey, just a few lines to let you know I am okay. I hope you are the same. How is everything by you?

Today is Sunday and all is well. I expect you will be going to church tonight. How are your spuds coming along? Are they doing good or not?

We had chicken. We roasted one hundred twenty chickens for dinner. I helped clean them and my hands are sure sore from the bones. I only work until noon today.

I was just out playing pitch and catch with the guys from my room. Do you remember Leo? He and I are still together. Not too may of the fellows we knew are in this outfit anymore. I guess time changes. It don't change my love for you though. Nor can it ever.

Well, as there isn't any news, I will close. Honey, you should be getting some of my letters by now. Well, Darling, give everyone my love and tell them hello for me.

May God bless you and keep you safe for me. Answer soon. From one who loves you dearly,

Your husband, Charles

Dearest Darling Wife,

Well Honey, just a few more lines to let you know I am okay and thinking of you. I am not getting my mail yet as I have only received a couple of letters from you for quite awhile. But it will start coming along soon. At least I hope so.

How are you and the children coming along these days? Are you all doing okay? How are your chickens? Have you lost any yet? I hope they grow good for you because one can never tell. Maybe I'll be home to help you eat some of them or at least some of their eggs. I sure hope so. Don't you?

Well, my dear, news is scarce and I am trying to do some washing and write to you. I will close and write more tonight. So God bless you and keep you and the children safe for me. Sending all my love and best wishes,

AS ALWAYS,
Your husband, Charles

Dearest Wife & Family,

Well, Honey, now that I got my wash done, I will write a few more lines. I just smeared something on me for the itch too. So now, I should be okay for awhile. I hope this finds you well and okay. I am okay so far.

Well, Honey it sure has been hot here today. I sure did some sweating when I was doing my wash. But I took a good shower so for now it is better. What have you been doing to try to stay cool? Drinking lots of coke, I bet. Have you had any candy bars and coke lately? I always laugh when I think of how you loved coke and candy bars. But I am glad we could have them, don't you?

Honey, I always remember the good times and fun we had together. We hope to have lots more when I get home, don't we?

So, Honey, I will close saying I love you from the bottom of my heart. God bless you and good luck. Sending you all my love, hugs and kisses,

Your husband, Charles

1945

Well, Honey, just a few more lines tonight as I haven't anything else to do or go.

Boy, I sure do get tired of just laying around. Time sure drags along. It seems to take forever for time to pass. It is just like wishing old age on myself, But to get home quicker I would like for time to fly until I get there. Then it can go just as slow as it wants. The slower, the better for us. The only thing, they won't tell us how long we have to wait.

Dear, I sure am fed up and tired of army life right now. Time did pass when we were in combat, but it doesn't seem to now. So instead of telling you my troubles, I will close.

As always from one who loves you with all his heart and soul. God bless you and keep you safe for me. Tell the children I said hello and for them to be good and help their mother all they can. Tell my folks to write to me. I love you. SWAK.

Your husband, Charles

1945

Dearest Wife,

Just a few lines to help me pass the time. I think they are going to have a show for us as soon as it gets dark. I think I will go if I think of it.

Honey how are your cows and chickens coming along? I sure hope you have good luck with them. Boy, I wish I had my dinner right now and I am not referring to the chickens if you know what I mean. Do you remember what I use to tell you in my letters when we were first married? Well I still get hungry for it. Do you? There are other things I want to but I will have to wait for that too. Haha

Well Darling, I had better not pout or put too much foolishness in letters. Every else is as usual, so I will close at this time.

From one who loves you heart and soul,
Your husband, Charles SWAK

Dearest Darling,

Well Honey, just a few lines to let you know I am okay. I haven't gotten any letters from you today so I will look for one tomorrow.

How are you and the children coming along? Fine I hope. How is your calf coming along. Is it growing any? How are the folks coming along? Are they well? What are they saying about the farm they bought? Are they going to build a house on it? He should have enough back in the woods to build a house and that is the first thing that should be built on the place.

So Honey, write and tell me the news. God bless you and keep you safe and well for me. Tell my folks hello and for them to write me. Give my love to the children. From the one who loves you dearly.

Love & Kisses

Your husband, Charles

Dearest Darling,

Well Honey, here is the first letter I've written in three days. We have been moving around. We moved to a new town but it is not as good as the one we were in before. But it ain't too bad.

Everything is as usual. No change of any kind. I still haven't got my mail yet. Boy, Darling, I hope it catches up with me soon. There isn't anything better than getting letters from your wife and home. Mail call is the best part of the day over here.

I am going to start cooking again at noon. Sure seemed funny not to have been cooking.

Well, Honey, I can't think of anything else to write about so I will close and write more this evening.

I Love You M y Darling,

Your husband, Charles SWAK

Dearest Wife,

Well Darling it is Saturday morning about 8 o'clock. So far it looks as if it is going to be a cool day. I hope so anyway. I got up and had my breakfast just now. I hope I get some letters today from you. I really do look forward to them.

Honey, what are you doing today? Saturday house cleaning I bet. Boy if I was home, could we get some house cleaning done. Haha. Honey do you reckon you could put up with me if I was home? I remember when we use to do things and you would get mad at me. Haha I wonder if you still would. Do you remember when I would fall asleep on Dillon Beach and you would have to come after me? I sure am a sleepy head ain't I? I also remember when I wouldn't answer the telephone and then you would really get hot at me, didn't you? Maybe I can do better if I am not in the army.

Well, Baby, I must close for now. God bless you and keep you well and safe for me.

From one who loves you dearly,

Your husband, Charles. Give my best to all. SWAK

Dearest Wife & Family,

Honey this is to answer your letter of June 25th and 29th that I just got today. I am glad you are okay when you wrote them.

Glad your chickens are doing good and I wish I was there to build a pen for them.

Now Honey, about you going home. You know it is okay by me. The only thing is if you are going I want you to go before the weather gets bad and makes the road bad. And I want you to be careful when traveling because if anything happened to you I would go crazy and I wouldn't have far to go there anyway as my news is going bad fast since I have been over here.

Honey, I am allowed eight packages of cigarettes a week. And I smoke that many. I would send you some, but someone would take them before they got there if I was to send them by mail. You will have plenty of time to get home before I get home as I don't think I will get home before six months or better.

So if you go be careful. From one who loves you dearly with all his heart and soul. Sending you all my hugs & kisses.

I love you, Charles SWAK

Dearest Wife,

Well, Sweetheart, how does this find you? It leaves me okay and longing for you.

I don't have much time to write just now because it is almost dark and we don't have lights in our room. I am living in an old garage. I figured it was better than living in those old bombed out houses. It hasn't got any windows in them. At least we got protection from the mosquitoes here.

I have to cut this real short, so my Darling I will say I love you with all my heart. I am going to bed now and think of you. Maybe I will have some good dreams. I hope so.

Sending you all my hugs and kisses. Tell the children to be good for me. God bless you and them and keep you all safe for me.

Your husband

Dearest Wife,

Here is hoping this finds you okay and well. I am okay, outside for a sore throat but it ain't too bad.

Boy, Honey, I was just sitting here looking out the window out over the valley below here and it really makes me lonesome for you. It looks a little like your Tennessee. I guess most of us over here are likewise lonesome. I don't have no idea when I might get back there but I am sure hoping it won't be too long. I sure would like to see you. I sure do get lonesome for you.

Well, I guess I am out of wind so I will close. Say, Honey, will you send me another pound of popcorn? I sure do get hungry for some.

Well my Darling, say hello to everyone for me. God bless you and keep you and the children safe and well for me. From one who loves you very much and think of you everyday and all the time,
Charles

Dearest Wife,

Well Honey, just a few lines to let you know that I am okay and thinking of you. Everything here is as perusual. No news of any kind. Just the same old stuff.

How are you coming along now? How are the children coming along? Are they well? Have you decided whether you are going home or not? How are the folks coming along? Working hard I would imagine. How is your livestock? Honey, even if the chickens are old and tough, we will still have a chicken dinner when I get home. Even if we do have to chew it a little longer.

Well, my Darling, I had better close this as there is not much I can talk about. Only that I love you and I can't tell you how much either. It wouldn't get past the censors, I don't think. But I do love you for other reasons too. It sure is plenty.

So God bless you and the children and keep you all safe and well for me. Tell everyone I said hello and to write to me. Your mail has not caught up with me yet but it will soon, I think.

So long and good luck, Charles I love you

Dearest Darling,

Well Honey, just a few lines to let you know I am thinking of you and hoping you okay. I am the same as usual. Okay and hope you are the same.

It has rained here for two days now here. I am going on duty at noon today. I am getting so I don't want to work at all anymore.

But, each day brings me closer to you., so I don't mind at all. Boy, I will be glad when that comes won't you?

Well, Darling, I've got to close and go to work, so God bless you and keep you safe and well for me. From one who loves you with all his heart and soul.

Your husband, Charles

I love you with all my heart. Answer soon. Sent with all my love. Do you still love me?

Dearest Wife,

Well Honey, just a few lines to let you know I am okay. I hope this finds you the same and better.

I got three letters, two old ones and one of July 22nd from you. I also got one from Burt and his wife. They are okay but they said they hadn't heard from you in a long time. Dad said Scott Andrews was over here somewhere. But I rather think he is in the Pacific as his A.P.O. is San Francisco.

Well, Darling there isn't much to say except I love you. Boy, when I get home I am going to give you such a loving. I can't wait. That is if you will let me. Will you?

Well, Dearest One, I will close. Loving you as always and always with all my heart and soul. God bless you and keep you safe for me. Tell our children hello for me.

I Love You

Your husband, Charles SWAK

Dear Sweetheart,

Well my little turnip and lump of sugar, how are you? I received your letter of the 28th. Sure glad to hear you are okay.

I am also glad you are willing to teach me to dance. Darling, we can really enjoy dancing with each other when I am home, just you and I. There is nothing I would love more.

Honey, I went swimming in the Rhine river yesterday.

Darling, I must hurry to get this in the morning mail. It is about six o'clock in the morning this Monday. I didn't write Sunday as I got up late. So my dearest I will close for now, saying I love you with all my heart.

I got a letter from Evie and Burt this morning. You remember them don't you? They got another baby boy now. We got some catching up to do when I get home won't we? Maybe two or three if we feel up to it.

I Love You My Darling,

Your husband, Charles SWAK

Dearest Darling,

A few more lines to let you know I am thinking of you. Boy I really get lonesome for you and keep longing to be near you again. You can bet when I do get to be with you again, I will never leave you, war or no war. I honestly believe that I shall be home before another summer goes by, possible sooner. Everyone here in this outfit thinks the same thing. So there must be a little bit in it. I hope so anyway.

So Darling, write and tell me how you are getting along. Tell me all about yourself and the news. Honey, ask my Dad if Bill Scherer ever got home or not. Did he make it through the war? I've been thinking of him lately.

So bless you my Darling and keep you well and safe for me. Sending all my love and kisses.

From the one who loves you dearly,

Charles SWAK Tell everyone I said hello.

Dearest Darling,

Well Honey, how does this find you? It leaves me okay.

I suppose you know by now that the war is ending over here. So you can stop worrying so much about me. Darling, I may not have seen as much of the war as others but nobody could be any happier to see it end. All I need now is to be at home. I certainly am looking forward to the day when I can be there permanently. Are you?

I just hope the Pacific War goes fast now. I guess the prayers you have been saying for me has been answered.

I will close for now. Tell all I said hello. Keep yourself and the children safe and well for me until I get there.

From one who loves you more than words can say,

Your husband, Charles XOXO

Germany May 30, 1945

Dearest Wife,

Just a few lines in answer to the letter that I didn't get yesterday. It sure is nice here today. Just a little cloudy, though.

I walked about twelve miles today. We had a flag raising ceremony for Decoration Day. People here made an American Flag for us so they raised it for the first time today. We baked a chocolate cake today and I am done until four o'clock a.m. Then I got to make about twelve gallons of cereal for breakfast.

Honey, I would like to know how much money you get each month now. Is it the same? Are you able to save any of it? I would just like to know how everything is going by you. Are you satisfied with the way you are living or not? Or do you have any ideas you would like to try? Let me know your general viewpoints on things concerning you, the children and me.

You know Honey, there is not much in those v-mail. I would like for you to send your letters air mail so you can write more.

How are your folks in Tennessee? Do you hear from them often and what do they have to say? How are the folks on my side? All well and kicking, I hope. Is Alice still in Green Springs with Sis? Has Jean ever visited you? Do any of my relations come to see you? I have asked you that several times but you have never answered. Do any of the people around there come to visit you? If so, who? The reason I ask these questions is that you never say. Whether they come or something like that. I mean just common everyday occasions. What goes on day to day. What you do or what you are going to do.

Have you ever become acquainted with the Rosses or the Scherers or any of the folks around there? You know I have not written anyone around there except for you and the folks for a month or two. And I won't until I can get you to write newsy letters to me. I would also like to know if anyone is making trouble for you. If so, who?

Do you remember that silk flower you gave to me? Well, it doesn't look like much now, but I still cherish it. Have you ever had your ring off yet? What does Jr. do these days? Did you let him have that girlfriend you wrote me about? Does Kenny come down to see you these days? Do you still wrestle with him anymore?

Well my Darling, I can't think of any more questions to ask. Do you still love me? If so, why? So answer a few of these questions at least. Namely, the last one.

Well Sweetheart, I will close at this time. God bless you and the children and keep you safe and well for me. Signing off saying I love you with all my heart. Tell everyone I said hello.

Your husband, Charles

June 1945

Dearest Darling.

Well Honey, how does this find you? Fine I hope. It leaves me okay. We had a real rain here today. I think I will try to find a place to swim tomorrow. What are you doing lately? I got about a dozen letters of yours today.

Say, what is that girl's name that Jim married? Where is she from? And did he come to visit when he was at home? How did he look? Was he as windy as ever? How long did he get off?

You said in your letter you only got one letter from me in four weeks. Well Honey, I am writing letters, but if they don't reach you, I can't remedy that.

How are the children? Are they still in school or had their vacation started?

Well, Honey, I must come to a close now. So God bless you and keep you and the children. Answer soon.

Your husband, Charles

Tell my folks to drop me a line every now and then. I would appreciate it.

June 1945

Dearest Darling,

How are you today? Fine I hope. This leaves me well and okay. How are the children doing? Are they out of school for the summer? How are the folks? Working hard on the farm, I suppose. I ain't heard from anyone for about a week now. I hope you ain't too busy to write me.

I just got through about two weeks of washing. Boy, I hate to wash my own clothes. I go on duty tonight, so I guess I will try to get some sleep this afternoon. I'll write you again tonight.

So, for now, I will say God bless you and the children and keep you all safe and well for me. All my love and best of luck to you. Tell all I said hello and for them to write me. And you keep me some letters coming on the way. You probably think I am a growling fool, but I really do miss getting your letters.

So, so long,
Love, Charles

June 1945 .

Darling Wife,

Well Honey, how are you now? I did write you last night but being in a hurry, it wasn't very much and being in a hurry, I didn't put much down very much. And what I did put down, I doubt you can read it.

We are having fairly nice weather for a change. We've had decent weather ever since we've been here. Would you send me some more popcorn please? Just a pound if you would? I could really eat some if I had it.

Honey, I think I will get out of the army alright. But, it is going to take some time, so don't get yourself all worked up. Anything could happen and I don't want you to be disappointed. I don't think you have to worry about me being sent to anymore combat areas, so that should relieve your mind some.

Boy Darling, I sure get lonesome for you. I guess that is one thing I would never get over. That's why I say, God bless you and keep the children safe and well for me. I love you with all my heart and sending you all my love.

Your husband, Charles

June 1945,

Dearest Wife,

Well Honey, how does this find you? Fine I hope. It leaves me fine.

Boy it sure is nice weather we are having here now. But, I wouldn't care if it were raining all the time if I could be with you.

How are our babies getting along? Fine I reckon and hope. I guess they are glad to be out of school. Boy, you don't know how I long for the day when I can be at home. I have your pictures handy at my bed and look at them all the time.

I guess the folks are mad at me for not writing more. But Honey, it keeps me busy just writing to you. My ambition ain't very high these days. Just hoping for the best and fearing the worst.

So, my little dumpling, I will close loving you with all my heart. God bless you and keep you and our children safe and well for me.

Your husband, Charles Love & Kisses

June 1945

Dearest Darling Wife,

I hope you are okay when you get this. I am okay. I received two of your air-mail letters today. And yes Honey, I believe I will get to come home but I don't know how long before I can get there. I still love you Darling, more everyday. I still keep the pink flower in my boot pocket. I always will. It brings sweet memories of you.

Yes, Darling, I think the idea that you and the folks have is alright. I think it is the best thing we could do when I get out.

I wish I could see that living room suite you got. Could you send me a picture of it maybe? I hope it is a nice one. What did you pay for it, if it is any of my business.

Well Darling, I must close for now. Tell all hello for me. Take good care of your self and our children for me.

From one who loves you more than he could ever tell.

I love you dearly, Charles

Dearest Darling,

Well Honey, just a few lines to tell you I am okay and hope you are too. Things here are as usual.

Honey I got an argument to settle with you. In one letter you say you haven't been fishing for a long time. That it is too hot to fish. That was written on July 23rd. In another letter you said you caught four pounds of fish. It was wrote July 3rd. Now, Honey, did you forget or do you call twenty days a long time. Haha

Boy, Honey, I wish twenty days was all I lacked in being home with you. Don't you? I hope you will keep that fishing date we have promised each other. I can at least catch a sucker on the wrong end of the pole. Haha. I know your morale is getting thin, but Honey, just hold on and keep your chin up and say a prayer for me and I will do the same. God will do the rest.

So for now, I'll say I love you. Answer soon. SWAK Some argument, huh?

Your husband, Charles

Dearest Wife,

Well, Honey just a few lines today to let you know I am lonesome for you.

I am okay and getting my mouth cleaned out pretty good. Boy, I hate to think I have something wrong with my teeth. It sure worries me. I guess I ain't use to having anything wrong with me.

Well, Honey, I really don't have any news on when I might get home. But it don't look too promising around here just now. I sure ain't there when it comes to having good luck. I always get the hard time connected to anything I get. But someday my luck is bound to change.

So Honey, until we meet again, I'll say I love you with all my heart and soul. Tell the folks I said hello for m e. From one who loves you,

Your husband, Charles SWAK

Dearest Darling,

Well, Honey, how does this find you? It leaves me okay except I have trench mouth again. I sure am lucky at getting things. But that is my luck, I guess.

I haven't heard any more about getting out. Looks to me I won't ever get out and I am getting pretty disgusted. My morale is only about knee high today. I wish they would kill all the Japs and Germans that ever lived.

But so goes life I guess. Some generations don't have to make the sacrifice of war. I just got in the wrong generation I guess.
Well Honey, I will write you this evening. I love you with all my heart.

Your husband, Charles SWAK

June 1945

Dearest Wife.

Well my little sugar lump, how does this find you? Well I hope. Everything here is okay.

We are in Belgium now. It is a nice country to be away from. I ain't heard any more about my points. So far my score is ninety-eight points and the score is eighty-five, so I am still hoping for the best. Things like that take time. So my darling, keep your fingers crossed for me.

Boy, Darling, I wouldn't know how to act if I did get out. I would be so happy. Darling this leaves me fine and thinking of dear ones, so I will close, loving you with all my heart. Tell everyone I said hello for me. All my love and kisses for you my dear. Take good care of yourself and the children. Bless you.

Your husband, Charles

June 1945

Dearest Wife,

Just a few lines to let you know I am okay and hope this finds you the same.

Sure is nice weather here. How is the weather there? What are the kids doing? Are they having a good time? I want you to let them have a good time this summer. Let Jr. have his fun, but don't let him go too far. Just to be sure he will be a good boy, too. I wish I could be there with you, too so I could be a good boy. Do you think I could be?

Well Honey, news is scarce so I will sign off and get ready to go to work this afternoon. Tell my folks I said hello to them and for them to write to me. So Darling I will say good luck and may God keep you well and safe for me. From one who loves you dearly,

Your husband, Charles SWAK

1945

Dearest Darling,

Well Honey, here are a few more lines this morning to let you know I am okay and thinking of you.

How are you this morning? What are you doing? I am just laying around putting in my time. It looks like it is going to be a nice day here. It sure is a heck of a place to spend so many nice days, but I guess it could be worse.

I haven't heard any more on my points yet. I've sent some of my clothes to the dry cleaner. Also four of my blankets. What have you been doing these days? Are you still figuring on going for a visit back home? If you are I want you to go before the weather gets bad, so let me know what you are going to do. It is okay if you want to go, just be careful for me.

Have you been fishing lately? If you have I'll bet you caught a sucker on the wrong end of the pole if you were. Honey, are the children doing okay and are they enjoying their summer vacation from school?

Well, I'll close, as news is scarce. God bless you and keep you safe and well for me. I am sending all my love and kisses until we meet again. I love you with all my heart and soul.

Your husband, Charles SWAK

Hello My Darling,

How does this find you? I am okay. We are having a nice day here for a change.

I did some washing today. I also got my field jacket out of the cleaners and sent a pair of wool pants and shirt to clean.

What do you think about us moving on the farm that Mom and Dad are on now? Do you think that would be okay? I think we could make a pretty good living there and we could get something better later on.

I would like to have your ideas on the matter. Do you think we could have a good home there or not? It is right close to Dad's and I could use some of his tools and machinery until we could afford our own. That is the main thing. It would cost like heck to start off to buy all our needs the first year or so. If we get things a little at a time, we won't feel the pressure or cost so bad. We won't need to go into debt all at once. So write and let me know what you think of the idea.

I went to a show today and Honey it was the one we saw together while we were in California. It made me think of the good times we had going to the movies then. We'll go to more when I get home. And please let me know if you go home and when you get back.

So God bless you and keep you. Answer soon.

Your husband, Charles.

Dearest Darling,

Well Honey, just a few lines tonight to let you know I am lonesome for you. It sure has been a nice day here. I took a shower but couldn't shave so will shave tomorrow. Everything here is the same. I am still lonesome for you.

I got my woolens back from the cleaners today. Did they ever do a poor job. One shirt sleeve was not pressed and one pair of pants was not pressed. So I guess that will end my business with the German laundry. I'll have to press them as you use to do.

I remember lots of things you did for me and I really appreciate them. Maybe I didn't show it like you would have wanted.

Well, Honey, I'll close for now and go to the show. So bless you my Darling and may God keep you safe and well for the one that loves you with all his heart and soul.

Your lazy old man, Charles SWAK

Dearest Darling,

Just a few more lines tonight to let you know I am okay and well. And that I am thinking so much of you and the children tonight. Everything here is okay and just the same. No news of any kind.

It is now two o'clock in the morning here and seven o'clock or past your time of day. The night shift ain't so bad if I keep busy.

Honey, put the children's full name and ages and birth date in a letter and send it to me. Also put it in the airmail letter, too. Then I will get it in one letter or the other. I need to turn it into headquarters. Be sure to send it as soon as possible.

Well, my Darling, I don't have much else to say as I haven't got a letter for about a week now, so I can't write much. Our mail hasn't got through since the last letter I wrote you. Maybe soon, I hope.

So I will close, saying God Bless you and keep you and the children well for me. From one who loves you with all my heart.

Your husband, Charles XOXO Tell all I love them.

Dearest Darling,

Well Honey, just a few lines to say hello and I am okay. Hope this finds you fine as well. Everything here is as usual, the same day after day. Boy I really get tired of it.

I had a dream last night. I was at home and was I ever taking life easy. But, boy, was I ever disgusted when I woke up and here I was, still in Germany. But I figured that was just my luck.

Well Honey, are things going as you would like them to go? Do you have trouble keeping busy? Or do you have trouble keeping too busy? I hope you have been getting my mail. I have been writing everyday and sometime two.

The army has a serious transportation problem right now. So slow mail can be expected.

So Honey, I will close for now. Say hello to all for me. God bless you and keep you and the children safe and well for me.

Your husband, Charles

1945

Well, just a few lines to let you know I am okay and hope you are the same.

Well Honey, I will answer the first letter I got from you with the new address on it. You wrote it on July 22nd. which was only eleven days coming to me. That isn't too bad. I am glad you are all well. This leaves me just as usual just lonesome for you all.

I am glad you are not tired of waiting for me as we might have a little time to wait yet. But, not too long I hope. Things are as usual here, no news of any kind. It has turned a little cool here. I sure am anxious to see you Honey, but I reckon just like you, I will have to wait.

What are you doing now? Are you still planning on going home or not? How are my folks? Are they all well?

Well, Darling I will close at this time, sending you and the children all my love. Tell the folks to write once in awhile.

Good night my Darling,

Your husband, Charles Answer real soon

Hello Darling,

I am answering more of your letter that I received July 22nd. Now Honey, I don't want you to be expecting me home before July of 1946, as it may be that long anyway. I would get there if I could, but I don't want you to be disappointed. See what I mean.

Honey, I never get tired of you saying you love me. You see that is what I have lived for. I'll give you a good spanking when I can for saying that. Haha.

I was all set on getting home for my twenty seventh birthday but that hope is gone. But the army can change overnight. I was sure a disappointed boy to be sure. It would have been wonderful if I had made it.

I hope your oil stove works pretty good. Honey, my itch is lots better. I work on it so I can get rid of it as soon as I can. Honey, when you address my letters, you are making a mistake. Be sure to copy it just as I write it. Okay?

I Love You, Charles SWAK

Dearest Wife & Family

Well, Baby just a few lines to let you know I am still dreaming of you. I hope you don't mind me calling you Baby, because you are my baby aren't you? I hope so anyway.

I just talked to a soldier who is going home Tuesday morning. He is flying back. Boy, was he happy! But I don't trust those planes even if they are safe. It sure would be a long way down if anything goes wrong up there. But, it is a long swim if the boat sinks. So I guess it is fifty-fifty.

Well, Honey, that is about all for now. Keep your chin up and don't get caught with your pants down. Do you remember those little step-ins I sent you that time?

Well Darling, a little foolishness goes a long way so I will close saying God bless you and keep you well for me. Sending all my love and kisses. Tell all I said hello and for them to write me. Tell the children to be good and for them to help you all they can.

Answer soon in a long letter. From one who loves you, Charles

Hello My Darling,

Well Honey, this makes three times I wrote today. So you see I have plenty of time to myself. I don't know how long it will last but for awhile anyway. Things are just the same here.

Men are coming home and other men are coming to replace them. So you see, I ain't getting no closer fast. I am sure, Darling, we will have our day sometime and not too distant in the future. I sure am lonesome for you today. I would give anything to hold you in my arms for five minutes. I think I could stand the waiting better.

But someday I am going to be able to hold you as long as I want and even you won't be able to stop me. Would you want to? Boy, Honey, I love you so much. No one could ever tell them how much.

Tell the children I said hello and give them a kiss for me and help their mother all they can. So Darling, I will close for now. Sending all my love. Tell all I said hello and write.

Yours forever and ever, Your husband, Charles SWAK

Dear Darling,

Well, how does this find you? Okay I hope. It leaves me alright.

It has been raining here for two and a half days now. How is everything going by you? Are you going home? I won't be home for quite a spell, Honey, so I don't mind of you go as long as you go before bad weather. If you haven't gone by October 1st, I want you to wait until next summer. If I get home by March, 1946, I will be doing good. So you got a spell of waiting, six or seven months at least.

So my darling I will just have to say I love you with all my heart and soul and look forward to spending the winter over here. They already have winter quarters set up for us so it is most true we will stay here.

So Honey, God bless you and keep you safe for me.

From one who loves you dearly, Charles

1945

Well, just a few lines to let you know I am okay. I've got to work this afternoon so this is the only time I will have to write.

Nothing about coming home yet. Boy, Darling, you don't know how I would like to be home. Would you like for me to be there or not? I hope so. How are the children? Are they alright? When are you going home? Let me know.

Well Darling, I am in a hurry as you can tell by my writing so I will close. So God bless you and keep my family safe for me. Sending you all my love. Answer soon.

Your husband, Charles

Hello My Darling,

Well, Honey, a few more lines to let you know I am thinking of you. And you can know also my dear that you are the only girl in the world for me. Darling I hope you believe me when I say things like that as I mean it from the bottom of my heart. You are the only one who could ever spoil it for me. I would die if I lost your love.

You may worry about me and the women over here but these women have never entered my mind as long as I can think of you and coming back to you. I am saying these things so you can put your mind at rest, if you haven't already a long time ago. And most of all so you may know I love you and you only.

May God bless you and keep you safe for me. I love you.

Your husband, Charles

Dearest Wife,

Well, Honey how are you now? It leaves me okay but very lonesome for you.

I am getting tired of sweating out my points. Sometimes I don't think the army is ever going to let us come home at all. It sure is taking them a hell of a long time. Always something else they need their ships for except sending the men home. I wouldn't be a bit surprised if they were sending the prisoner's of war home before they send their own men home. But I guess if most of us live long enough we may get back sometime.

Well, Dear, I can't do anything but gripe and that doesn't make for good reading. I will close

God bless you,
Your husband, Charles

June 1945

Dearest Darling,

Well Baby, how does this find you? Fine & dandy I hope. The weather is nice over here right now, not too hot and not too cold.

I went out to the garbage dump today. The German people were there, eating the bread crumbs and other slop as it came out of the garbage can. Boy Honey, I sure hope nothing like that ever happens in America. You don't know how lucky you are. Some of the German people might deserve it but I don't think little kids should have to go through that as they are not at fault.

Well Dear, as I ain't got much news now, I will sign off. Tell the folks I said hello.

From one who loves you dearly,

Your husband, Charles God bless you and keep you safe for me.

June 1945

Dearest Darling,

Well here is another letter to let you know I am thinking of you.

You know, Honey, I've just been sitting here and thinking and wondering if you are going to teach me to dance by your radio. That is if and when I get home. I often think how I use to want to dance with you but didn't know how. I don't think there is anything wrong with dancing as long as you do it at home. We have had quite a few dances since we've been across, but I still have my first dance to go to. So you see I haven't learned to dance yet. So if you won't learn me then I will just have to go to dance school. Haha.

I just sit here and listen to the radio music and dream of you. It makes me so homesick. It seems the closer it gets to me coming home, I get more desperate inside to come home to you.

God bless you my Dear, sending all my love and kisses to you. From one who loves you dearly.

Your husband, Charles

1945

Dearest Wife,

Well just a few lines to let you know I am okay and thinking of you.

Say, I bet the kids are good at catching fish. Did you get any suckers? Haha.

You said that Harve and his wife dropped in to see you. I hope all went well. He is such a razzer at times and you can't take him seriously.

Another thing, even when I get my points, it will still be quite awhile before I come home. So don't go getting yourself all excited because you are going to be let down. I want out as bad as you want me out but I will just have to wait my turn. That looks to be a long time off.

So my Darling, I will sign off, asking God to keep you well and safe for me. I love you with all my heart and always will.

Love and Kisses, Charles

June 1945

Dearest Darling,

Well Honey, how are you today? As for me I am okay.

I got a letter from your folks. They are okay as well. Everything here is as usual. No news on the points as of yet. I guess I'll be forever getting out of here. But Boy, I can still hope.

What are you doing these days? Do you still go to church? Or do you go at night? How is it now that school is out? Do you have any time for yourself or not? Are the kids having a big time? I hope they do because they won't be young forever.

Well, Honey, I must close for now. I am out of news and it is getting late.

So take care of yourself, sending all my love,

Your husband, Charles

June 1945

Dearest Wife,

Well Honey, just a few more lines to let you know I am okay. I hope you are okay as well.

I received two letters from you. Was glad to get them. I also got one from Mom.

Well Darling, I got a new A.P.O. number so be sure to use it? It is A.P.O. 758. Everything is unchanged except for that.

Boy, my darling, I sure do get lonely for you. It seems a long time since I last saw you, especially from one whom I love so dearly.

How are the children? Have you caught any more fish? Honey, you and I have a date to go fishing together the first chance we get when I come home. Haven't we? I'll bet I can catch more fish than you. Haha.

Well, Sweetheart, I will close for now. From one who loves you dearly and only wait until I get back to you.

Your husband, Charles

June 1945

Well Honey, how are you ? It leaves me okay.

Yesterday was Sunday and I went swimming. Sure had fun. But it made me tired for not being use to it. The water was nice. Honey, when I get home, you, the children and I will go swimming together. That will be wonderful, won't it? I think so anyhow.

How are you coming along? Are you doing okay? What are you doing to keep your morale up? Mine isn't up to par and isn't worth heck these days.

Well, Darling I must close for now and say God Bless you and keep you well and safe for me. Is my popcorn on its way? I hope so. I really get hungry for some.

I love you with all my heart and soul. Answer soon if not sooner.

All & my love and Kisses, Charles

July 1945

Dearest Wife & Family,

Well, Honey, just a few lines to say I am okay and lonesome for you.

The boys had a dance here last night and it was a real blowout. I went up and looked on for a little while. I would not want my wife to act like those women did. Outside of that, things are the same.

Boy Honey, I get more tired and restless everyday. I have to wait dear but I would love to swing by your place and get loose.

I got about half a sore throat now and I still am not making much headway on my itch. So outside of that and sweating, I am okay.

Are you going home or not? If you do, please be careful for me. Tell all I said hello and to write to me. From one who loves you with all his heart and soul.

Your husband, Charles

June 1945

Dearest Darling,

Well Honey, I got four air-mail letters from you today. And was I ever proud to get them.

No Honey, you don't need to worry about me getting mad at you. I am glad for you to be able to get what you want. I would be a poor husband if I got mad at you for getting stuff what you want. The coat and dress that you got in San Rafelo was different. You could have asked me first, but didn't. So you remember that. Haha.

While I am away from you, just do as you think best and there won't be any kick from me about anything. The only kick I have now is not being able to get back home to you.

Well, Darling I will close, saying God bless you. Tell all I said hello.

Love & Kisses, Charles

July 1945

Well Darling, here is a few more lines to let you know I am okay and thinking of you. Things here is as always.

Boy do I get tired of waiting around. I wish I could be at home where I could do some good for you as well as for myself. Haha. I had a good dream of you last night. I only wish I was living it instead of dreaming it, don't you?

Now, have you been having a good life? Honey, I got two letters from you, one from July 9th and one on the 6th. You said we would have chicken to eat when I get home. Honey, they may be pretty tough by that time. But we can eat them anyway. Haha.

Honey, three hundred sounds like an awful lot for the furniture. But if you are happy with it, it sure is okay by me. I guess you would have a hard time making a picture of it for me so let it go.

First, remember that I love you and always will. Sending my love to the best girl I know and want to know. I love you with all my heart.

From your husband, Charles SWAK

July 1945

Dearest Darling,

Well Baby, a few lines to let you know I am okay, just thinking of you. Everything here is as usual. No news of any interest.

Well, my Dear, I have been here for two weeks and haven't got no mail as of yet. I will probably get it in bunches. I really can't kick on your letters as you have really been a faithful writer. Lots more than your lazy husband. I have always told you I wasn't much good when it came to letter writing. I hope you don't hold it against me. I will try to make it up when I get home.

How are the children these days? Tell them hello for me and for them to be good. How are my folks doing? Are they fixing up that house? I hope they don't plan on moving into it with the shape it is in. What are they figuring on doing? Do you know?

Well, my Darling, keep yourself well and safe for me. From the one who loves you with all his heart,

Your husband, Charles Answer soon I love you SWAK

July 1945

Dearest Darling,

Well Baby, how does this find you? Okay and swell I hope. It leaves me alright.

It has turned out to be a very good day here. I just got back from the doctor's office. He gave me more stuff for my itch. It isn't getting any better but it hasn't gotten any worse either. At least for now it stays about the same. A lot of the guys have it here so I am not the only one who catches things.

How are the children coming along? If you go home, I want you to be careful and don't get into any accidents, especially while traveling. Because I am going to be plenty worried until I get the message you are back.

Honey, my nerves sure are bad. And I can't figure out what is causing it. I don't drink at all and I don't smoke anymore than usual. I guess worry about coming home is doing it and worry over the itch, too. I'll be glad when this is over and I will be at home where there will be peace again.

I love you with all my heart and soul, Charles

July, 1945

Dearest Darling,

Honey, a few more lines to say I am okay. Hope this finds you the same and better.

It sure is hot today. I'll bet it is hot there as well. I am listening to the radio as I am writing this. They have lifted the No Fraternizing Ban, but there is only one lady that I want to frat with. If you think hard enough you may know her.

Well Darling, I can't think of much to write. This leaves me okay and lonesome for you. With God's help we will be together soon.

God bless you, my darling,

Your husband Charles SWAK

July 1945

Dearest Darling,

Well, Honey, here I am again. Haven't got much to say but will write anyway.

Everything here is about the same. I have got quite a sunburn. I hope it will turn into a tan. July is not a good month to lay out in the sun I don't think. Do you lay out in the sun any?

I am not making much headway with my itch. When I get home and if I could get hold of the right stuff, I will clear it up fast. Medicine is scarce over here. I will get it cleared up someway.

Boy I sure get tired of just sitting around. How are things by you back there? Are you working hard? How are your chickens? Are they growing any? How many did you buy? Have you got any that is laying now or big enough to eat?

Well, Honey, I will sign off now. God bless you and keep you for me until I get home.

From one who loves you dearly,

Your husband, Charles XOXO

August 1945

Dearest Darling,

Jr. said his mom was playing the piano. I didn't know you could play the piano. Is Jr. going to learn to play his accordion?

What have you been doing these days? Are you raising a big garden this summer? Does Jr. help as he should or does he just get in the way? Haha. Do you have any trouble getting him to work? Boy, Honey, I wish I were there to get in your way. I sure would like that. Would you?

Well my darling, write and tell me all the news and just how you are coming along. Good night, God bless you and keep you safe and well for me.

From your husband Charles, who loves you with all his heart. You'll never know just how much I love you.

Tell everyone I said hello and to write to me.

I love you Dear, Your husband, Charles

1945

Dearest Darling,

Well, I will try to answer your four letters that I got today. One was written in June and the other July 4th. I sure was glad to get them and know you were okay. I am always doing that, just thinking of you and wondering how you and the children are.

Honey, you know your buying the living room suite doesn't affect my love for you. I am glad your chickens are coming along okay. That sour milk is good for the chickens, I guess.

Honey, I got plenty of points. The only trouble is finding a ship to come home on. They are needed for other things. I haven't got the least idea when I do get to come home. It may be six months or a year. So don't go looking for me for at least six months.

Yes Honey, I· will be very good when I get home or I would try anyway. The only reason that I love you is that I love you. Haha. Ain't that all that matters? Honey, to me you are the swellest and sweetest girl I know. I am glad you got your suite. I hope you like it. I hope you will always be proud to wear that ring as I do yours.

Honey, do you still go to church? And oh yes, be sure to let me know when you go home and when you get back so I won't worry. It is hard to worry so far away.

Honey, tell my folks I would like a letter from them for a change. You take care of yourself and don 't work too hard. I will close and hope to get some mail from you with my new address on it soon. Tell my children I said hello and for them to be good and help their mother all they can.

So, God bless you and keep you well and safe for me. I am sending you all my love and kisses. From one who loves you with all his heart and soul.

Your husband, Charles SWAK

Dearest Wife,

How are you? Fine I hope. I am thinking and longing for you.

I got more sores on my back today. I hope I can get rid of those pimples by getting more of a suntan. Honey, I think I have gained ten pounds in the last month. But I ain't any too fat yet. I guess I am just going to be a slim jim. But that is okay as long as I am well and okay.

Have you gained any weight since I left? What are you doing and how are you getting along? How are the children? I'll bet they have suntans.

Well, Darling, I don't have much in the way of news so I will close. So Darling, keep praying and I will do the same. With God's help and some good luck, we will be together sometime soon.

Charles SWAK

August, 1945

Dearest Wife,

Well, Honey, I got your airmail letter today. Glad you are okay. Things are as usual over here. No news as to when I can get started home. But my guess is it will be some time yet. If I get home to start spring planting, I will be lucky.

I ain't making much headway with my itch. It sure give me fits at night. I have it on my stomach and legs. I sure hope I can keep it from spreading. I doctor it all the time. I wish I was there for you to doctor it. I bet it would heal fast then.

Honey, it is a blue Monday and it sure is blue for me.

God bless you and the children and everyone else back there. I love you all with all my heart.

Your husband, Charles I love you, I love you, I love you.

Dearest One,

Well, Darling, it is raining hard here and it sure makes me blue for you.

I talked with an officer and he said that would surely be home in five months. I was really hoping to be there for my birthday, but I guess I was having pipe dreams. I can say it will really be nice when I do get to come home, won't it?

Anyway, they asked me if I wanted to enlist for another three years. Honey, as far as I am concerned, they could have asked me to go jump in the ocean. I wouldn't enlist again for a General's pay.

So, Honey, you take good care of things for me and when I get home, you can take good care of me. Haha

This is the first letter I have written you in seven days. I hope you are not angry with me.

Yes, Honey, I will go to church with you anytime. My nerves are a lot better, but I can't promise not to worry. I can't help that. I am glad you are going to wait until we can go together to see your folks. It will be great to be with each other and with our children.

I am glad Betty is going to school. I bet she will be a good little scholar.

Well, Honey, I worked very hard today and I am very tired, so I am going to bed. Tell my dad to have a place for us of some kind because I will be home to work. I ought to be there in four or five months at best. I hope so anyway.

So God bless and keep you for me,

Your husband, Charles

Karlsbag, Germany

August 19, 1945

To a Girl that needs a Spanking,

Well, Honey, I got four letters from you today and in two of them I am really surprised at you.

No Honey, I have not forgotten what we mean to each other and I love you a million times more than I did. I didn't mean anything when I asked you if you would like to be single. I meant it only as a joke but I always must remember that I have a wife that don't take to joking. Anyhow honey, even if you did want a divorce I wouldn't let you have it.

And as for putting an order for a baby, well, Honey, I have the order blank all filled out and ready to mail. Only I am a long way from the one I need to have me mail it to. And Darling you shouldn't even have to guess who that might be. Do you think I could get her to help me fill the orders and get them mailed off? That order has been waiting ever since I left her. She can be sure of that. She will see when I get home.

I am glad you are canning up food for winter. It is a real good sign of a good wife. I have never doubted you are a good wife. In my opinion you are as good a wife as a man ever could have. Anyway to me you are.

Well Honey, I have quit laying in the sun. It seems only to make my itch worse as far as I can tell. A fellow asked me the other day if I was allergic to wool. I guess I never thought of that.

Honey, time sure drags when a person is just waiting. My darling, I will be so happy when I get home. I get homesick for the good times we use to have. I will never forget them. They are so valuable to me.

God bless you all and tell all I said hello.

Charles SWAK

August 1945

Dearest Darling,

Well Honey, I just received two letters from you today and was I ever glad. This leaves me fine, only lonesome for you.

I am leaving my outfit tomorrow morning. I turned in my rifle today as I am going to an outfit that has mostly high points men in it, so I won't be in the infantry much longer. I will send my address as soon as I can. I sure hope it won't be much longer. But one thing for sure, I will not be shipped to a combat zone. So you can rest at ease over that.

Just save a place in your heart and Honey, I will be there as soon as I can. I am anxious to be a husband and father and I am really going to try and do a good job of it.

So Darling, I must close and check all my clothes and equipment for leaving. It sure will seem funny to leave men I have been with and known for the most part of four years.

God bless you and keep you well for me. I love you with all my heart and soul.

Your husband, Charles

Dearest Darling,

Well, Honey, how are you today? Fine and dandy, I hope. As for me it leaves me okay but lonesome and longing for you. I had a dream about you the other night and was it ever good.

We are moving again to some other town, here in Germany. We are to do occupation work the rest of the time we are in Germany. I will let you know as soon as I know what town we are in.

Anyway it will break the monotony of waiting to come home. Boy, the time can't pass soon enough for me. The sooner it passes, the sooner I get home. But, it will seem like five or six years instead of five or six months. They said we would be in for the duration and I think they are right.

Anyway, when it is over, I know that I will get home, and believe me, I look forward to it. It is the brightest outlook I have had for some time now.

So, Darling, be patient and I will do the same. God bless you and keep you,

Your husband, Charles

Dearest Darling,

I am writing so you will have my new address. Be sure to use it from now on. How are you? I am okay.

It sure seems strange to be in this new outfit. But all the guys here have eight-five points or over so I guess this is the place to be. I sure hated to leave the old outfit, but I don't think I would like the place they may go.

Well, I will write more later. We are back in Germany now, in a town called Augsburg, in the central part of Germany. Look on the map to see where I am located.

So, for now, God keep you safe and well for me.

Love & Kisses,

Your husband, Charles

August, 1945

Well Honey, just a few lines this evening to let you know I am okay. Everything is fine here and I guess I will get along in my new outfit. I hope so anyway. I would like some quicker action in coming home, though.

I took my blanket and laid out in the sun today and did my belly get red. My back didn't get too much. I am going to try to get a real good suntan. I am real white from working in the kitchen.

I am okay but I got the itch again. That stuff must love me. I get it every time I turn around. I am trying to stop it before it gets very bad this time. The doctor gave me some sulphur to help cure it.

What are you doing this evening? I don't reckon you have any trouble keeping busy. What I wouldn't give to be home again. But it won't be very soon though, I don't guess.

So my Darling, I will close. I hope to hear from you soon. God bless you and keep you well for me.

From one who loves you with all his heart and soul. Your husband,
Charles SWAK

Dearest Wife,

Well, Dear, just a few more lines to let you know I am thinking of you and am trying to make up for the days when I didn't get time to write.

There sure is a lot of differences in this outfit from my old one. Everyone here has lots of time for everything. I sure hope it stays like that.

Baby, it is Sunday and a nice bright day and I would like to be spending it with you.

How are the children coming along? Fine I hope.

Yes Darling you are not the only one who would like to have one of those nice long kisses we use to have. They really were swell. Anyway, I thought so. When I get home I am going to have lots and lots of them, ain't I? I am looking forward to that anyway.

I miss you like nobody's business. God bless you and keep you safe and well for me.

All my Love and Kisses,

Your husband, Charles

Dearest Wife,

Well, Darling, how are you tonight? As for me, I am okay.

Boy, Honey, some of the boys went fishing today and came back with about fifty rainbow trout. I fried them up and was they ever good.

What did you make out with your fishing? Have you caught any more? How are the folks making out on their new farm? I'll sure be glad to be there to help them with the spring planting. At least that is what I am hoping for.

Honey, I hope you aren't getting tired of waiting for me. Are you? I don't think it will be as long as we thought. So just keep your chin up and if it is God's will, I will be there before very long.

So God bless you and keep you and the children well and safe for me until I get there.

I love you with all my heart and soul,

Your husband, Charles SWAK

Dearest Darling,

Just a few lines to let you know I am coming along. I am still trying to get a suntan. I saw the doctor this morning and he told me to stay out of the kitchen until I got rid of the itch. So I guess I won't cook for awhile. Boy, I get into the dangest messes. I'm always getting something.

How are you coming along? Are the children okay? What are they doing there these days? Everything here is as usual. I will be so happy to walk down the street in civilian clothes again. Lots of guys are leaving here each day to go home but I am getting nowhere fast. It may be some time before I even get started for the states. But I will get there sooner or later. Think you could put up with me if I got home to stay? Wouldn't that be nice? You wouldn't send me back to the army would you?

You know I love you, but just to be sure, I'll say I love you with all my heart and soul.

Your husband, Charles SWAK

Darling Wife,

How does this find you? All okay I hope.

Boy, I hope Japan quits as it looks like it may. Sis won't have to worry about Carl as well as many others will be at ease also.

Honey, could you tell my dad that I am thinking about his offer of letting me have the farm he is on now. I would like to take over for him anyway as he is getting ready to retire, anyway, or should be. I think I will stay there right on the farm he is on now. I would like to buy the farm if the owner would sell at a decent price. But I doubt he would sell for what the place is really worth. You and I will decide those things when we are together again, won't we?

I love you my Darling, Charles

August 10, 1945

Dearest Wife,

Well, today is a great day isn't it? I heard Japan surrendered and all is well. Now people can take a deep breath. Honey it is too good to be true. I sure hope it lasts. Our commander was speaking to us a while ago. He told us we should be on our way home in a short time, now that Japan gave up. Boy wouldn't that be swell? I just hope that it is true and not a pipe dream. I just can't seem to get it in my head that it is all over. It sure is a good thing for Carl and Sis too.

I hope what the colonel said is true. If it is I will be seeing you sooner than I thought I would.

So God bless you and keep you and our children well and safe for me. HONEY I AM COMING HOME!!!

To the sweetest woman I know. From one who will always love you, forever.

Your husband, Charles SWAK

My Darling,

Well just a few more lines to let you know I am okay.

Time sure drags when you are waiting to get started. We should be leaving for our new A.P.O. in a few days or so. We will be there for a week or ten days and then we will start our long way home. But I won't mind, as I will just be that much closer to be home with you.

But this never seems to pass. I hope we get on one of the Queen's ships as it doesn't take them very long to make the trip. The other ships are slow. I've got one and a half days to work in the kitchen and then I am finished. I hope I don't have to cook on my way home, as I am really getting tired of cooking.

How are the children and you coming along these days? Are all three children going to school? How does Betty like school? I bet she is in a class by herself. I bet you are lonesome in that house all by yourself while the kids are in school. But you will have me soon to put up with. And then you won't be lonesome then. Haha.

Well darling, I will close for now. God bless you and keep you well and safe for me.

Your husband, Charles

Hello Darling,

Well Honey, just a few lines to let you know I am okay.

I am leaving tomorrow to start the process of coming home. Boy, I hope I don't have to go through some of the B.S. other boys are going through. I hope when I start, I can go straight through instead of having to wait all along the line.

I have to get up in the morning and get breakfast for all the men. I hope that is the last meal I have to cook in the army. Everyone here thinks we are going to be making a fast trip, even the officers. So you see I am hoping for the best.

I've got a sore finger. It is the little one on my left hand. I think I have an infection in it, but I think it will be okay.

Well, Honey, I can't think of much else to write. I've got water on now heating so I can wash and shave. It is hot now so I had better get busy.

Honey, keep your fingers crossed and say a prayer with me and with God's help, I will be there before very long. Maybe I'll be there before those chickens get too old to eat. I sure hope so.

From one who worships you. May God bless you and keep you well. From one who loves you dearly,

Your husband, Charles

Dearest Wife,

Just a few lines to let you know I am well.

My finger is coming along just fine now. I had to soak it in salt water to get it to stop swelling. We are having inspection today. I hope it will be the last we have. They are suppose to be here soon so we can go to our new A.P.O. It can't be too soon to suit me.

I think we will be in the port around the 5th or 6th of September. We will go through a lot of medical exams and inspections there and get more shots, I think. Then right on our boat.

Just how long, I don't know. They told us we could have our own choice of waiting for our discharge or waiting on our discharge and trading for a thirty day furlough with pay. Then we return to get our discharge. I am going to take the thirty-day furlough, as it will be just another month's pay. There isn't any catch to it. We get our discharge when the thirty days are up. I guess it is a good idea. I can't make money any easier. What do you think?

Well, God bless you and keep you well and safe for me.

Charles

Darling Wife,

Just a few lines to let you know I am okay and to say hello. How are you? My finger is still sore but getting some better. We are having a time over here. We are seeing some very interesting sights. And boy, Honey, I would rather be home. I sure am fed up with army life but so are lots of us.

I am now in 255th infantry. Seems like a good outfit. I had to sleep on the floor last night but I don't mind as each day brings me closer to you.

Well, you can look for me in October. Boy, Darling, that isn't long is it? This time it is to stay. No going away anymore. Boy, oh boy, oh boy! Isn't that going to be grand? You tell Dad and Kenny to get their guns oiled up as when I get there you and I and them are going hunting. At least for a half day or so.

Well, this is what you and I have been waiting for. You know Who to thank for it. We will thank Him together as soon as we can.

We are having rainy weather here now, but I don't care as I ain't here for long now. Boy, I sure am happy. Now I can be with you all the time. Isn't that going to be swell? There isn't use for you to be writing because I ain't going to be anywhere to get mail any more. But I will write every chance I get.

Boy, Honey, you won't need to cut wood for this winter. I will be there to cut it for you. Honey, I am just as happy now as anyone can get in the army. Just knowing I am on the way HOME!

We are due in port between the 1st and 5th of September. So with good luck, I ought to be in the U.S. in October. Now Honey, if this is the last letter you get, don't be disappointed. I will be moving constantly but always toward coming home and our happiness together. We've been waiting for so long. We've been waiting for so long but I won't have any time to write you. You know, I will come straight home to you as fast as I can get there. So don't be worried about anything.

Just take real good care of yourself and be careful for me. I hope this is the letter you have been waiting for so long. I know it is the letter I have been waiting to write, telling you I am on my way home to you.

So Darling, say hello to everyone for me and God bless you and keep you safe.

From the ones who loves you dearly,

Your husband, Charles

P.S. Tell Dad to start planning on what kind of deal he is going to make me on the farming business. Sending you all my love

August 24, 1945

Dearest Wife & Family,

Well this leaves me fine. I hope it finds you likewise.

It won't do you any good to writes me as we will be moving around so much that it won't get to me.

I am still looking to be home for my birthday. Sending all my love and best wishes. God bless and keep you.

Your husband, Charles

Epilogue

October, 1945

The little girl climbed up the ladder to the hayloft of the small barn to look at and play with the newly born kittens.

She glanced out the large open space where hay was brought through and saw a car slow down and stop. She watched intently as a tall man in uniform got out, opened the back door and took out a big bag and heaved it to his shoulder.

He turned to shake the hand of the driver who waved to the soldier as he drove off.

The soldier stood quietly for a moment looked around at his surroundings and then started slowly toward the house.

The little girl caught her breath and whispered, "Daddy, Daddy! Daddy's home!" She scurried back down the ladder and ran out to greet him.